SMALL HOUSE BIG STYLE

Better Homes and Gardens® Books · Des Moines, Iowa

CONTENTS

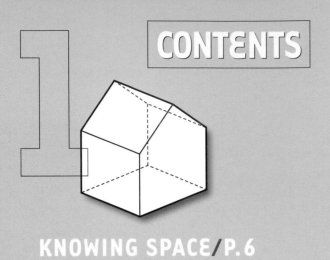

KNOWING SPACE/P.6

WHAT'S YOUR STYLE?/P.24

SMART REMODELING/P.114

GAINING SPACE/P.156

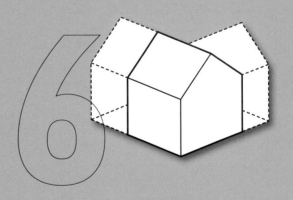

Better Homes and Gardens® Books, An imprint of Meredith® Books
Small House Big Style
Editor: Paula Marshall
Contributing Editors: Susan Andrews, Cynthia Bogart, Andrea Caughey,
 Nancy Ingram, Rebecca Jerdee, Bonnie Maharam, Elaine Markoutsas
Associate Art Director: Mick Schnepf
Copy Chief: Catherine Hamrick
Copy and Production Editor: Terri Fredrickson
Book Production Managers: Pam Kvitne, Marjorie J. Schenkelberg
Contributing Copy Editor: Jane Woychick
Contributing Proofreaders: Kathy Eastman, Susan Sanfrey, Tricia Toney,
 Diane Witosky
Contributing Photographers: King Au, Ed Golich, Tria Giovan, Bob Greenspan,
 Jenifer Jordan, Janet Masek Macke, Emily Minton
Contributing Illustrators: Carson Ode, Daniel Pelavin
Indexer: Kathleen Poole
Electronic Production Coordinator: Paula Forest

Editorial and Design Assistants: Kaye Chabot, Mary Lee Gavin, Karen Schirm

Meredith® Books
Editor in Chief: James D. Blume
Design Director: Matt Strelecki
Managing Editor: Gregory H. Kayko
Executive Shelter Editor: Denise L. Caringer

Director, Retail Sales and Marketing: Terry Unsworth
Director, Sales, Special Markets: Rita McMullen
Director, Sales, Premiums: Michael A. Peterson
Director, Sales, Retail: Tom Wierzbicki
Director, Book Marketing: Brad Elmitt
Director, Operations: George A. Susral
Director, Production: Douglas M. Johnston

Vice President, General Manager: Jamie L. Martin

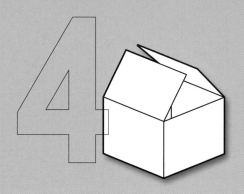
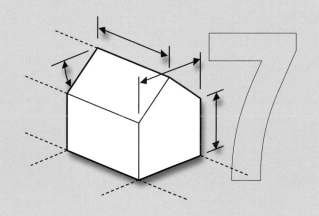
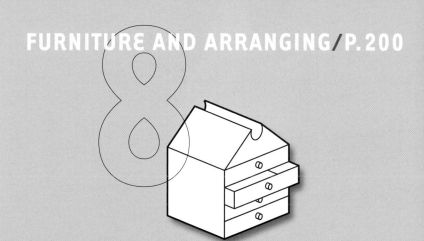
Better Homes and Gardens® Magazine
Editor in Chief: Jean LemMon
Executive Interior Design Editor: Sandra S. Soria

Meredith Publishing Group
President, Publishing Group: Christopher M. Little
Vice President, Finance & Administration: Max Runciman

Meredith Corporation
Chairman and Chief Executive Officer: William T. Kerr

Chairman of the Executive Committee: E. T. Meredith III

All of us at Better Homes and Gardens® Books are dedicated to providing you with information and ideas to enhance your home. We welcome your comments and suggestions. Write to us at: Better Homes and Gardens Books, Shelter Editorial Department, 1716 Locust St., Des Moines, IA 50309-3023.

If you would like to purchase any of our books, check wherever quality books are sold. Visit our website at bhg.com.

I have always lived in small homes, from the 1000-square-foot ranch house that my parents bought the day I was born (where, incidentally, they still live) to the 1700-square-foot saltbox my husband and I live in today. While I sometimes longed for more space in those houses—and in the dorm rooms and apartments where I lived in between—I came to understand that more space isn't the answer and that wisely using available space eases many a crunch.

In this guide for living well in small homes, you'll find hundreds of ideas for adapting to your space—and for making space adapt to you. The first two chapters follow the old advertising axiom of perception as reality: Space can be made to look larger or smaller than actual dimensions suggest. These chapters are lessons in seeing the space of a home and understanding your spatial preferences.

The next five chapters show how to use the elements of home decorating, remodeling, and building to make the space feel just right for you and your family. The examples include simple, readily accomplished changes and long-term projects that require devotion and vision to see them through. The final chapter offers advice on furnishing a small house—how to choose furniture pieces and where to put them.

Of course, the personality of any home is a most important feature. The compliment that most warms my heart is when friends say they see my personality reflected in the look of my home. The people who live in the small homes featured in this book overlaid their personalities on the walls, floors, and ceilings of their homes, imbuing the structures with a unique life and vibrancy. Use the ideas in this book to do the same in your small house.

Paula Marshall

Paula Marshall, Editor, Small House Big Style

Why does one small house feel comfortable and airy while another house of the same size seems crowded and cramped? It's how a space is perceived that makes the difference. Three elements—lighting, lines of sight, and a sense of height—help

KNOWING SPACE

create that perception. Along with smart storage and good furniture arrangement, these elements make any house live to the fullest of every square foot. The two diverse homes featured here show how the three elements work together.

CALIFORNIA DREAM ISLAND

/ Coastal Contemporary /

650 SQ. FT. The first step to stretching the space in your small house is to stretch your mind: Learn to see the space and the potential it holds.

San Diego architect Lew Dominy saw possibility where others saw a triangle of dirt. He built a house that respects the location and uses every square inch to maximum efficiency. The essential elements he used are not closely guarded trade secrets, but they do require a practiced eye. Look carefully at the details; the work of a clever hand is evident throughout. Dominy's use of light, height, and lines of sight offers many ideas that will help you stretch space in every room of your home.

The lot is just 90 feet long and 26 feet at the wide end, tapering to point at the other end. No typical house, full of right angles, would fit. Nor could the house be two stories straight up: A tall house would block the neighbors' ocean view and appear top-heavy. The solution came from the sea. Dominy took design cues from the floor plan and flowing curves of a ship.

Below

You are *here*. Really. The only empty near-beach lot in tony Del Mar, California, was on a traffic island. An architect with vision and tenacity figured out how to build a house on this sliver of land. Sometimes space, like beauty, is in the eye of the beholder.

Below and Right

The only unbreakable rule of small home design is to adapt. To accentuate the ocean view and to create privacy, the big-window living room and kitchen are up top; solid walls with glass block windows "below decks" reduce glare and noise in bed and bath.

The living room and kitchen on the upper level open up with wraparound windows bringing in sunlight and the ocean view at treetop level. In the kitchen, the highest interior location, the view looks down on the street, reducing the impression of being right on the pavement while still scooping up a view of the ocean.

Curves are crucial to making the space visually flow. The gentle wave of the ceiling and windows in the living room, for example, gives the eye a longer, uninterrupted "trip" that maximizes the perceived space.

Where's the color? A few bright accents punctuate the space, but the overall tone is deliberately muted for harmony. Glass tabletops keep the light and view flowing.

Opposite Left

With near-beach property, often the best way to see the sea is from a height. This deck is perched up top for just that reason. A solid wall, vs. an open railing, provides a touch of privacy as well as being an all-important safety feature. Also, the house essentially has no yard, so including this outdoor space was crucial to making the house live well.

Above

Too many dramatic features in one small space can create a visual tempest in a teapot. Here, the sweeping ceiling and window lines are given their due dominance. The furnishing pieces—subtly toned furniture, open shelving, an airy coffee table—along with muted colored walls and floors blend and add visual interest with texture.

Top Left

Unless they're Claes Oldenburg sculptures, electrical switches, plugs, and outlets are best kept unseen. Tucked into the window's overhang these necessities are unobtrusive. Recessed halogen lights also function fabulously without grabbing undue attention.

Middle Left

The solid wall behind the dining area breaks up a wall of windows and defines the space. A ship's portal enlivens the blank surface, allows in light and air, and creates visual interest. The built-in dining table and bench (see next page) are also ship equipment.

Bottom Left

This electrified appliance garage helps everything fit in a condensed space. Low-profile appliances add to the space's efficiency, readily sliding out when needed. Imagine the opportunity lost if this space had simply been left open and without power.

Above

The lines and curves in this house are admittedly quirky. In the kitchen, corners are not right angles, the windows are curved. Square rooms wouldn't fit the lot. Playing with the geometry distorts the perspective and increases the feeling of spaciousness.

Left
The living room-kitchen-dining areas are the
ultimate example of sharing, a line-of-sight
thing that works with lighting and height. The
light and views flow unobstructed from space
to space; the varied floor-to-ceiling
distances define individual spaces but keep
the open feel.

Below
Even the space below the dining-area
seating cushions has a job. Special-
occasion serving pieces slip neatly into
these cubbyholes.

Bed and bath are on the lower level where light and sight can best be controlled to maintain privacy; solid walls also muffle the traffic noise. While the height in these rooms doesn't need to be generous—private spaces often benefit from a sense of coziness—adequate light could have been an issue. Here, a slim band of windows circles the top of the space to solve the problem. A gently sloping ceiling (11 feet at the bedroom door, 9 feet at the bathroom) exaggerates perspective in the space making the room appear deeper, and thus spacious. In the bath, glass block protects privacy while allowing in light. All three elements work in concert, and light ties the spaces together.

/A LESSON IN LIGHT/ All the elements work both ways: Each can shrink or expand perceived space. Light isn't about having lots of it; it's about having the right amount in the right places so you don't feel as though you're living either in a cave or on stage. Look at what light does in your house:

Left
Well-chosen, smartly placed items make niches work well. Built-in swivel lamps mean reading in bed is a non-glaring situation. And the cube of electronics adds ambience and does alarm-clock duty.

Left
Good design addresses life's practicalities. Tucked a half-story below the dining room table and in the guest bath is the front-loading laundry space.

Above
How does a design incorporate everything in a teensy space without claustrophobic clutter? Keep the view smooth: A surround of cabinetry visually recedes while the mirrors and a ring of windows borrow space and light from the adjacent spaces.

/ Look at each room in all types of lighting situations, from bright sunlight to lamp-lit late night. Decide whether a room feels too bright or too dark at any time. Then look for the things that skew the view: dark corners, light fixtures that look too high or too low—anything that creates "hot spots" or weird shadows that need attention.

/ Note where sunlight enters a room and what it does at different times of day. Bright light pouring through a picture window in the morning can be joyfully bright or a retina-burner that needs to be tamed with shades.

/ Consider the absence of sunlight too. At night, black-hole pictures window can be softened with a wash of light from small overhead fixtures.

/ How deep does sunlight reach? Hallways can be dreary even on the brightest days. Lamps, overhead fixtures, or even skylights may be in order.

/ Think of balancing and blending. When the light fades before reaching the far wall, a room will appear smaller; even a small lamp on a far wall visually moves the wall out. Shadows aren't intrinsically bad; they just need to make visual sense. Strong contrast between light and dark is tough on the eyes. Dimmers, low-wattage fixtures, and smart placement allow you to balance the light.

/ Note how light carries from space to space. A bright hallway fixture that burns like a Kleig light into a bedroom should likely be noted for replacement.

/ Carry a small lamp on your room tours. Place it in the dark spots and turn it on. Does that help? Admittedly, a small lamp may not provide sufficient light, but it's an easy way to estimate the effect of change.

Above
In this tiny, practical corner, there are six different surfaces. Because they're all complementary to each other in texture and tone, visual harmony prevails.

Left
In houses large or small, a light in front of a mirror is a good thing. It creates a reflective synergy that makes wattage go farther and enhances the perceived space.

Left
Underbed storage needn't be old boxes shoved in with the dust bunnies. Built-ins like these are elegant, efficient, and dust-free for life.

/ Design Flash /
Note how the trim at the base of the mattress connects to the adjoining furniture. It's a subtle way to keep your eye following a line and making the space visually flow.

EAST COAST CARRIAGE TRADE

1400 SQ. FT. Most dream houses are created within an existing basic house shape—remodeling. Be aware: Meshing dream with reality gets messy. Castles in the air float easily, but even Cinderella, who coped so graciously with fireplace ashes, would have reached wit's end had the plaster dust started to fly.

John Kean, head of an architectural firm, knew the Long Island waterfront location made a tiny carriage house worth turning into a comfortable home. So he did. Twice. After the first remodeling, the transformed structure was a suitable home even when baby made three. However, 16 years after Kean purchased the property, when baby two made four, it was time to remodel again.

The plan initially called for simply adding a mudroom lined with cabinets for storage. But, as often happens with remodeling, the project's scope expanded. He and his wife eventually made improvements throughout the house. The result is a home of practical elegance and classic architectural style. It functions well for the family and makes the most of this ideal location. Good use of sight and height maximize the feeling of space.

Opposite
French doors bring in daylight and a waterfront view. At night, drapes provide privacy and the transom allows a peek of the skyview. A peaked ceiling follows the roof line, maximizing the room's height.

Below
Tweaking tradition maintains style but makes this home live large. Bay windows stretch space and view, transoms and skylights bring in light and add height. The rooftop and windowtop areas add fair-weather rooms.

For all the newness, this revamped cottage uses some time-honored elements. Lots of carved molding, paneled walls and wainscotting, and traditional furnishings give the house an established, historical look. By paying close attention to the scale of the rooms and keeping the spaces open, however, the Keans and their architect left the tightness of old houses behind. Clever thinking—the powder room door on the stair landing, for example, is paneled just like the surrounding wall—blends modern conveniences right into the style.

/LINES OF SIGHT/ Maximize the perceived size of a small house by visually sharing space from room to room and from the outdoors to the indoors.

/ Follow through—or not. Using the same colors, molding, and flooring weds one space to another; changing defines

Left
Judicious use of deeper hues helps shape a room of light colors. Here the dark wood elements punctuate the room, and the furniture's neat blue piping gives the eye something to follow.

Above
A bay window is an excellent space stretcher. The span of windows brings yards of the outdoor view into a room and offers bench seating that doesn't take away an inch of floor space.

Top Right
An unusual solution adds whimsy to a classic arch detail. The railing dips to frame the view of the chandelier from the upstairs hall. Windows at the top of the wall along the stairs open up the space.

spaces as separate. The view from family room to mudroom mostly matches: The wall color and wainscoting are the same but the flooring change defines the difference.

/Consider interior options. Extend the view between interior spaces with windows. Topping a bedroom door or wall with a transom window maintains privacy while opening up the view. French doors between the bedroom and a home office allow you to close up shop at day's end without closing off the view.

/Frame exterior views. Consider the view to the outdoors before bringing it in. A tree-filled backyard is a delight to behold in any season. Driveways, busy streets, and a neighbor's window just a nose away are better left outside. Use big windows and minimal window treatments to maximize the good views.

Opposite
For bay windows, the bigger the bow, the more it can hold. Here, the architecturally detailed arch brings the casual, dinner-for-six niche up to federal-style standards. Extra chairs can be pulled up to the dining cove or turned to the conversation area.

Above Left
The remodeling plan all started here: a mudroom with storage. By paying attention to details—color, cabinetry, skylights, and plenty of coat hooks—the space functions well and looks stylish.

Above Right
In a house this small, no place is ever truly out of sight. Here, a built-in bench and oval window make the most of the line of sight from the kitchen and family room.

/ Design a picture-perfect view. Less-than-perfect views can sometimes be salvaged. Translucent sheers allow just a peek of the outdoors, curtains hung halfway up a window cover an unsightly street but bring in the treetops, and up-top transom or clerestory windows provide privacy with a view. For windows with the worst placement, there are etched-glass designs or sky scenes on translucent plastic that adhere to the glass. Although the scene doesn't change, the impression of an expanding view still comes in.

/A SENSE OF HEIGHT/ Look up. How close does the ceiling feel to your nose? If it's too close, changing the actual height may be overly difficult, but there are ways to make the ceiling keep its distance.

/ Break it up. Even if a house has unvarying 8-foot ceilings throughout, the sense of height can vary. A continuous bright white ceiling tends to visually rise, while a rich color can bring it closer. Paint the entryway ceiling a deep neutral, and the white ceilings in nearby rooms automatically rise. Wide, arched passageways also break up the constant height.

/ Side-by-side comparison. One way to make a ceiling rise is to make the ceiling next to it appear lower. When a kitchen ceiling visually drops down with a soffit or deep molding at the ceiling, the adjacent family room looks taller by comparison.

/ Go down to go up. Varying floor depth affects the feeling of height above. An entry hall that's a step or two higher than the living room adds an expansive note.

/ Add a light from above. Adequate lighting near the ceiling also keeps it well above your head. Recessed lights, track lights, and torcheres keep the ceiling from becoming one big shadow at night.

Opposite Left

Adding decorative elements and a light to the backdoor overhang makes the family entrance as inviting as the front door. Curved, leaded windows in and above the door bring light and a view of the backyard into the house.

Below

With a kitchen this small and open, appearance is as important as function. The peninsula, does triple duty: storage, food prep, and eating. It also gently separates the kitchen from the family room; the end cabinet on legs softens that line.

Opposite Right

The over-sink mirror reflects light and views, expanding the sense of space. Behind the mirror is a medicine chest. Many medications need a constant temperature not found in steamy bathrooms, so putting a medicine cabinet in the kitchen is a wise choice.

Right

The architectural focal point over the stove covers the exhaust system. The display cubby in front matches the built-in cabinets that flank the kitchen wall. The upper cabinets are hung a tad lower than normal to make the top shelves easily accessible.

Think of a room most comfortable, the kind that compels you to enter.

Remember, this is your dream, so it's *your* idea of what is inviting. What words

describe how the room feels: open or snug, spacious or cozy? Focus on how the room

WHAT'S YOUR STYLE?

feels rather than the particular furnishings within it. From there it's not rocket

science to figure out your style preference. Follow the cues in these homes to

create the rooms that embody your sense of comfort.

AIR APPARENT

/ Breezy Ranch /

| 2750 SQ. FT. |

Open style is a good choice for mid-20th-century ranch homes. For example, even a once down-and-out post World-War II house readily sings a Moderne tune. The basics were built in: Lots of big windows for light and sight, long lines of sight between rooms and down hallways, and peaked ceilings emphasizing height.

Real estate agent Nancy Rothman trusted the instincts of her favorite designer, Daen Scheiber, when he said that a few alterations would stretch the open feel of the house: A wall between dining room and living room, typical of the home's era, cut up the floor plan. Removing this wall achieved a sense of flow, and the clever decorating that followed enhanced the open space.

Right
A plethora of windows visually annexes the patio to the indoor living areas. Furnish the outdoors as carefully as the indoors to keep the harmonious feel.

Opposite
The curved sectional sofa is as sweeping as the view. Floor-to-ceiling windows and strategically placed plants blur the line between indoors and out.

Opposite
Removing a wall between the living room and dining room made both feel much larger. View and light now flow freely between. The large opening also allowed room for the piano. The dining room is minimally decorated, keeping the emphasis on the living room.

Below
An open floor plan that's decorated in contemporary furnishings can play up the geometric angles, causing an overly harsh appearance. This room is softened up by a curved sectional sofa and a round coffee table in the seating area. Full, floor-length draperies soften the edge of the big corner window. The large mirror above the fireplace is a key view extender.

ight, sight, and height are maximized with neutral tones on walls, floors, and window treatments. This palette provides a perfect backdrop for an eclectic collection of new modern pieces and Rothman's favored family furnishings. The clean lines of the built-in shelves draw little attention and set off the striking objets d'art.

/OPEN SESAME/ Creating an open feeling in a small house requires finding, then going with the flow. Think minimal detailing, extend views, and maximize light.

/Carry on. Use a single, light-color palette on the walls and ceilings throughout connected areas. Whites or pale neutrals work best. Keep trim details spare and of a light color, and continue them from space to space.

Left
Travertine tiles cover both the hallway floor and the patio, blurring the line between indoors and out. Transom windows allow privacy and bring light to the bedrooms. A rug at the living room entry is both practical—catching dirt at the patio door—and aesthetic; it defines part of the space and, along with the angled chest, keeps the hallway from looking like a long, white tube.

Opposite Top Left
Tucked behind the dining room, the den is furnished in softer, more casual pieces than the main living areas are, but the streamlined architecture matches the living and dining rooms to maintain the feeling of openness.

Opposite Top Right
The home's crisp, light background recedes, so almost anything goes for furnishings. In this corner, a French farm table, topped with Asian ginger jars, fits in because it shares the home's simple lines and nothing else in the room visually fights with its deep color.

Opposite Bottom Left
The master bedroom accommodates a diversity of styles. A custom Spanish-style cabinet sits peaceably next to a modern side chair. The chair's quiet tones, curve of repose, and lowness contrast the cabinet's tall, firm lines and deep tones. The room also shows the freedom that comes of a restrained hand: A few well-chosen furnishings make as strong a style statement as a room stuffed with items.

Opposite Bottom Right
The white bedroom exudes serenity. The tone-on-tone approach of several shades of white creates warmth and avoids the stark feeling that can come of too much white. The bed has a padded headboard and tapered square legs. The bed's soft lines complement the strong geometry of the classic 1930s Eileen Grey glass and chrome side tables.

Opposite
Originally, a lumpy peninsula divided the long galley kitchen; now the job is done with changing styles. The kitchen has a sleek and efficient look with simple white cabinet fronts and streamlined handles. The dining area pops with pattern and color in the banquette. The separation of window groups simultaneously widens the space and defines the two areas.

/ View through. Make the most of the view to the outdoors with windows and few, simple window treatments. A clear view between interior rooms is also important to create an open feel. Remove doors where possible or widen passageways from room to room.

/ Down in arms, up in legs. Furniture that's leggier looks more open; so do chairs and sofas with thin, low, or no arms and backs.

/ Turn an eye to the sky. Light-colored ceilings with minimal texture and simple molding visually rise. Add light sources from above, too, to keep the sense of height at night.

/ Define rooms with details. Use a light hand to apply spots of color: Area rugs, pillows, or even a few dark pieces of furniture anchor a space. Intermediate tones can be used more generously but still judiciously. Wood cabinetry in a smooth, rich hue adds warmth and character. Tone-on-tone fabrics, or simple repeating prints work well to maintain an open feel.

/ Maximize light, day and night. Keep open rooms well lit so that the far walls are always clearly in view.

/ Store more. Open style doesn't mean jettisoning the stuff of life, but putting some away improves the view. Smooth front, built-in cabinets "hide" well along walls.

/ Lean into the curve. A few curved furnishings or walls help soften hard angles. Curves also visually extend a room, making it appear just a bit farther from here to there.

STYLE/FILE

/ Put a Little Cozy in Open /

To keep a house with an open floor plan from feeling cavernous, make a room snuggle up a bit. This kitchen has lower beams, a painting of darker hues hung above, and a dark wood cabinet—items that conspire to create a cozier feeling even though the kitchen's width and height match the expansive dimensions of the adjoining living room. The connection between the spaces is maintained with a flow of white walls and wood floors.

Creating Rooms with an Open Feel

O pening up the style of a room starts with an exercise in subtraction. Imagine the room bared to the walls, clad only in a demure coat of white paint. Then introduce color and furnishings sparingly, and stop one step before the room seems finished. That last element would likely be a step too far. The view to adjacent rooms then needs to be cleared, too. The kitchen here and the rooms on pages 36 and 37 show what happens when the visual bumps in the road are removed or smoothed.

Left
The curvy swervy open shelves put attractive serving pieces on display and at hand. The shelves wave the line of sight at each end of this kitchen, blending the view into adjacent spaces. Perched on stainless-steel legs, they float above the floor and look more like furniture than cabinets.

Above
Smooth needn't be boring. The fronts of the large storage cabinets, with their varying sizes, shapes, and finishes, create a pleasing backdrop while performing a day-to-day chore.

Far Left
From the back door, both eye and foot can readily travel through this remodeled kitchen. The path is clear, the view unobstructed—classic open style with a retro beat. The room has four windows and five doors that dictated the layout.

Left
Smooth fronts on appliances and cabinets broaden the vista and reflect the light.

Above
Soapstone caps the cabinetry in an unbroken line. It's a smooth choice to pull together the door and drawer fronts, open shelves, and windows. Custom-made cabinets make the view more interesting and avoid the dull repetitiveness of stock cabinetry.

Top Right
Cutting the wall by the basement stairs in half helped ease the room's tight feeling but stole a storage cabinet. Maximizing other storage areas, however, ensured no loss of capacity.

Middle Right
Sleek appliance fronts keep the look and feel on an even keel. Serving and cooking pieces that are best stored in vertical storage slots are readily at hand over the oven and microwave, but a smooth-fronted cabinet conceals their uneven appearance.

Bottom Right
Yes, this kitchen is in this house! While the spirit of the 1950s is evident in the style of the kitchen, the cookie-cutter influence is completely banished. The kitchen's dimensions were unchanged by the remodeling: $16 \times 11\frac{1}{2}$ feet.

NOTEBOOK

Above

This modern house shows the expansive effects of maximum light, height, and sight. A spiral stair anchors the entry, wood floors warm the cool starkness. Horizontal elements—exposed beams and curved overhang—and immediate openings to adjacent rooms keep this entry from feeling like an elevator shaft.

Top Right

Prevent a feeling of being lost in space by anchoring the room with furnishings. Using few and subtle tones in this living room adds visual weight, and gathering all the pieces around the rug by the fireplace grounds the arrangement.

Below Right

A stairway opens up with light colors and an airy metal railing. Maximize room openings along stairways to ease the squeeze. If not enough rays reach the space, add wall sconces, a strip of track lighting, or picture accent lights to illuminate artwork and steps.

Open style rooms have elements that are clean, and the rooms sometimes are sparsely furnished. The emphasis is placed on simple forms and clean architectural lines.

Above

Rhythm can be putty in the hands of someone with a good eye. The repeating doorway openings frame the view to the outdoors three rooms away. A bright chair and low cabinet interrupt the view so the path flows rather than races to the distant window.

Top Right

Traditional does open style in this dining room. The table doesn't need to throw its weight around because the surrounding furnishings visually step back in light tones and open framework. The rug defines the space, the vine pattern keeps the touch delicate.

Bottom Right

Even a teensy bathroom tucked into the eaves can visually open up. All the tricks are used to great effect here: glass shower doors; a humongous mirror; lots of natural and artificial light; light, smooth surfaces; and generously sized floor tiles.

COZY EXPECTATIONS

/ Cottage Ranch /

Above
No surprise here. This all-American cottage became the perfect setting for a newlywed couple to decorate in a comfortable, casual, cozy style.

Opposite
From living room to dining room, the color shift is dramatic, but the transition is smooth because the tones are similar. Deep, solid wall colors emphasize the playful combination of prints on the furnishings.

1900 SQ. FT. From the Department of Obvious Conclusions: Many small homes lend themselves to a cozy decorating style—and sometimes following the obvious can be the path to fabulous personal style.

Susie and Sean Brennan knew at first sight that their quirky cottage—with a step up or down between some rooms and a meandering floor plan—had room for everything. Following the house's lead, they filled the rooms with color, pattern, and cozy furnishings to make a cottage style statement. Solid colors on the walls hold together this gathering of many things: The palette of rich, earthy colors is repeated in the many prints on the pillows and upholstered pieces. The wall color changes room to room, allowing for a distinct feel in each while maintaining a sense of connectedness between spaces.

Reversing a long-held decorating rule, the smallest rooms—kitchen and bath—are wallpapered in large-scale floral prints, making them feel even cozier. The touch of bright in the prints also balances the deep solid tones of the adjacent rooms.

A good sense of visual balance is required to make cozy style work. If the words "Stop me before I chintz again" ring true, approach this style with caution. A little pattern goes a long way in a small room. Start with one or two prints in keeping with the color pallet; adding more prints is always an option. Balance curvy florals with geometric stripes and plaids; anchor with solid colors.

/COZYING UP A SPACE/ Rooms that wrap around like a hug define cozy. Here are some key ideas for creating the look:

/Turn down the lights. A cozy room may have as many fixtures as an open room, but richer colors absorb the light. Print lamp shades, and voluptuously curved lamp bases also "cozy down" the wattage by dispersing the light. Dimmers mechanically create the effect.

Top Left
Because there's much to look at in cozy styles, the focal point fireplace gives the room a needed visual center. Bookcases and benches flank the hearth for an extra dose of warmth.

Top Right
Lighter yellow tones and rustic accessories give the family room decor casual appeal.

Left
Decked out in striped wallpaper and outdoor gear, even the base of the stairway has an individual style. The mirror's reflection makes the most of available light.

Opposite
A wall of windows and light-colored walls and fabrics open up the family room to accommodate furnishings that carry a cozy feel: a large entertainment center, pine storage chest, and big, plush furniture pieces.

/ Design Flash /
Footstools are the perfect small house accent. They provide extra seating, extra table space, and napping spots for the cat.

Above Left
Smooth white cabinets, countertops, and appliances provide the backdrop for the visual activity of the wallpapered ceiling and a collection of decorative plates. The wallpaper cozies up the kitchen without making the small space feel crowded.

Above Right
A garden window captures an abundance of sunshine and allows a bit more room for creative expression. Topiary herbs add to the outdoor feeling and help to screen a direct view to the neighboring house.

Opposite
The boldly colored walls are cooled by touches of blue and white, big windows, and neutral fabric on the wing chairs. Benches on two sides of the table are a flexible seating option and give the room a needed touch of openness.

/ Create close quarters. Move sitting pieces close together to create a feeling of intimacy. Footstools, side tables, and a generous coffee table make lingering in soft chairs more enjoyable.

/ Go down and out. Speaking of the sitting pieces, many of the coziest pieces of furniture have full, fluffy cushions, high backs, well-rounded arms, and they hug the floor with ruffled or pleated skirts or short, stocky legs. These beckon someone to sink down into them and relax.

/ Boldly go with pattern and color. Choose rich tones and a balance of patterns. Remember, while pattern adds much to cozy, too much can create visual chaos. A large, all-over floral print on a high-back sofa needs room to breathe. Otherwise it can overwhelm a room.

/ Fill the view. More is often better to up the warmth and cozy of a room—more photos on chock-full bookshelves, more pillows on the overstuffed sofa. The only word of warning is to stop short of a creating a dizzying feeling.

/ Restrain the sights. Views to adjoining spaces both indoors and out are always wise in a small house. In a cozy small house, use generous or even elaborate window treatments that extend beyond the window. These choices create a cozy feeling without restricting light and sight.

/ Think of rooms as vignettes. By changing colors and textures from space to space, the view is shortened—you can still see from room to room but the changes accentuate the shift to a different room.

/ Go bold with molding. Deep cove molding painted in a contrasting color keeps the ceiling at a comfortable height but doesn't overly elevate it. Deep baseboard and window moldings complement the ceiling detail. If new molding isn't in the budget, paint existing molding in a contrasting color to give it punch. Wallpaper and stencil borders are effective alternatives or additions to molding. Excessive use of these can, however, easily overwhelm, so restrain the urge to do every room.

/ Honor the basics. In a room with a lot of visual activity, give the focal point its due to give the eye a place to start taking in the view. Work outward from this point to create a visual path.

/ Go mobile. To keep the look fresh, choose a few versatile pieces that can move from room to room—footstools that add seating or table space, pillows that complement chairs in two rooms, and even lamps that add refreshing light in different places.

Below Left

The guest bedroom is a restful blue. Each room is independent, so a big swing in tones is expected. The mix of fabric remnants, vintage textiles, and bedding creates a symphony of pattern and color. Furniture with simple lines doesn't compete with the patterned fabrics.

Below Right

Just a touch of gingham, a classic cottage pattern, hung from simple Shaker pegs, is all that's needed to cozy up the window. Look for spots that need little flourishes like this to finish up a room.

Opposite Left

Removing the door to the medicine chest and putting in a framed mirror, contrasting wallpaper, and a small lamp add much needed light. The light is magnified by a second mirror on the adjacent wall that's surrounded by a painted picture frame.

Opposite Right

Texture is as important as color in painting a vivid vignette. The subdued tones of the embroidered, crocheted, and chenille pillow covers add another dimension of visual interest to the many patterns on the chair.

/ Put a Little Open in Cozy /

Teensy-weensy kitchens gain needed visual elbowroom when dressed in open style. This kitchen opens up with tall cabinets, vertically striped wallpaper, and plenty of light from an unadorned window. The iron-legged table adds counter space without blocking the view. Dim the light and the kitchen recedes, allowing an intimate atmosphere in the elegant dining room.

NOTEBOOK

Making Rooms Convey a Cozy Feeling

Going cozy involves embracing some of the quirks that make small houses feel snug. Nooks, dormers, tiny rooms, and angled spaces have a celebrated place in the cozy house. The essential principles of decorating are interpreted closely: Furniture sits close together and walls visually move in a bit for coziness. Add plenty of pattern, texture, and color to create a depth of views. The kitchen here and the rooms on pages 48 and 49 exemplify the fullness and detail of cozy style.

Left
Although newly remodeled, this kitchen has the appearance of being original to the house in almost every detail—cabinets, flooring, fixtures, and appliances. Modern times peek through quietly, but so subtly that the look is uninterrupted.

Above
The antique-style stove has generous proportions and deep colors that requires the rest of the room yield to its dominance: The cabinets across from the stove balance the deep color but are lighter in build. The light-colored walls and middle-tone flooring are also comparatively light in appearance.

Far Left
When this house was built, kitchens were seen as work spaces, not showy spaces.

Left
Following through to the details makes all the difference. The curvy faucet, deep sink, and arched backsplash maintain the look of cozy cottage style.

Above
The small dining area at the center of the L-shape room opens up with light colors and big windows. Floral prints and pillows keep the cozy flow and invite lingering. Including fabrics in a kitchen also helps absorb some of the clatter of pots and pans in action.

Top Right
Surrounded by cabinets, the refrigerator is tucked around the corner. Given its own space to dominate, the fridge doesn't crowd the main area.

Bottom Right
Beaded board on the walls flows from space to space, and a gentle arch softens the view. Freestanding pieces like this hutch of a complementary style add to the old-fashioned, "unfitted" kitchen look while serving practical needs.

/ Design Flash /
The pantry-style cabinet is actually built into the space between the wall studs, making it deeper than it appears and able accommodate many sundries .

NOTEBOOK

Above
Cozy takes on a lightweight look. The bones of this back porch are quite plain; the warmth is all from thoughtful decorating. Using leggy white pieces lets light and sight pass through. The white, slanted ceiling never dips too low, and the rich green walls neatly set off the lively furnishings.

Top Right
Keeping the feeling cozy without getting claustrophobic can be tough in a hallway. The line of the battens in the hall paneling extends to the ceiling. The space stays enclosed while light flows through. Switching from white tile to wood flooring warms the space.

Bottom Right
Understair storage often blends into the wall. Multi-paned glass panels in the doors and wicker baskets convey a pantry look. Tiny framed prints complete the effect, making this a place of cozy cottage charm rather than just another blank space.

Every room has cozy potential. Even the boxiest space with little intrinsic inspiration can become a warm, snug space. The secret lies in layering the details.

Above

This nook is a quirk of design in a modern tract house. It becomes a perk by using a tiny-pattern wallpaper that reflects the larger print in the main part of the room and adding luscious curtains. An inviting wing chair, a simple window seat, and scalloped-edge tea table make this a spot for relaxing.

Above Right

Sometimes creating cozy means following the path already laid out in a room's design. Extending the deep lilac color all the way up the sloped ceiling snugs up the space. The restful color is repeated in the quilt and prints on the iron bed.

Right

Often the smallest rooms in small houses, bathrooms often default to white to maximize the feeling of openness. To cozy up this space without causing a closed-in feeling, use a simple, rich color scheme and balance with white. The generous floor-to-ceiling shower curtain maintains a feeling of height; putting the light fixture into the ceiling also adds visual height.

Your personality is rich with color and texture; your rooms should be too. In a small house, however, these powerful elements can seem intimidating. Take a deep breath and boldly go forward into homes where people dared to challenge the

COLOR AND TEXTURE

myths, celebrate the rules, and tweak the options of using color and texture in small houses to create a highly personal flair. Then move forward with confidence to use these tools to create the style and feel that express your personality.

MIXƎD MƎDIA

1500 SQ. FT. Take a moment to ponder this possible scenario: What if you could write the rules for designing and decorating a small house? You'd probably keep some basics: Rooms for sleeping, meals, socializing, and personal care are necessary for the house to function. And light, height, and sight are essential to make any house live well. But without the inhibition of perceived rights and wrongs, how the rooms are placed and defined would change. With open-ended rules, how materials are used becomes artistic expression as well as function. And for the most daring artists, few rules need apply.

Using just three original walls of a rundown bungalow as their "canvas," Tracy and Kim Stearns created just such an artistic, new-rules house in rural Kansas.

Right
Clad in corrugated galvanized steel, the exterior has an ultramodern farmstead feel to it. The steel adds just enough glimmer and texture to be interesting but not glaring.

Opposite
The kitchen cabinetry is a freestyle gathering of recycled pieces; the unexpected is expected.
/Design Flash/ The window molding is picture framing—to frame the view.

Opposite
Furnishings and wall colors define rooms while the floor flows on. Oriented strand board (OSB) is a common subfloor, but here it's painted like checkerboard tiling and covered with polyurethane. It's a perfect background: adding visual interest without dominance—and it's durable and inexpensive.

Above
The stairway floats across the yellow supporting arch, depriving the living room of neither light nor view. Imagine how closed off and dark the room would have been if the stairway were enclosed. (The last visible remnant of the old house, the fireplace, holds a quiet corner position.)

Left
The house is designed to offer a series of views, through the inside and to the outside. There aren't a lot of windows, but all windows and glass doors are generously sized to bring light and outdoor views deep into the house.

The Stearnses' home squeezes the most fun into function. Bright colors and mismatched items give the house a playful feel, but everything has a job. A bright yellow arch goes from the first floor to the roof; but it's not there just for artistic expression: It encloses the ductwork for the heat pump and is a structural element that holds up the house. The arch also allows the floor plan to be wide open, with few interior walls.

The home reflects the Stearnses' design philosophy. As a commercial designer, Tracy has made the clever use of materials part of his trademark style. As a bonus, the style is also cost-effective: Many items are secondhand finds and building materials all dressed up.

/GOING ECLECTIC/ Assembling a singular scheme from a bunch of disparate items takes practice. Tracy offers these tips for mixing it up with flair.

/ Follow your heart with patience. This style isn't built in a day. The couple gathered items over time, then worked

/Design Flash/
The spare bedroom is just a nicely appointed bed in the corner. It's the 95-5 rule in action—the house is designed for how the couple lives 95 percent of the time, adapting for the 5 percent of the time company comes. The open loft gives guests the feel of staying in a weekend cabin. Screens stowed along the closet wall slide over to provide a modicum of privacy.

Opposite
The feel of the sleeping loft is subdued but the fun plays on. The big yellow arch reaches to the peak. Cool industrial carpet (for comfort underfoot and noise abatement), white walls, and warm wood accents turn the tone serene.

Top Left
A grid of textured glass windows is all that defines the master bedroom; light and view easily carry through to the adjacent space. Moroccan-style lights add an exotic note.

Top Right
A long, lean custom cabinet runs along the knee wall, visually elongating the space and providing storage and display areas.

Left
Even the top-of-stairs hallway functions with style. Skylights and a round window draw light to both levels. Plain closet doors emphasize the perspective of the space.

Opposite
According to conventional thinking, the choice was generous windows or a two-sink vanity. Creativity won out over both: Freestanding dual sinks go back-to-back, with a photography studio pole doing mirror, towel, and waste bin duty. The recurring themes of oriented strand board and metal also appear.

to fit them into the house. The kitchen island is a salvaged store display cabinet.

/ Embrace the perfection of imperfection. Part of the joy is in the home's unpolished look—the mosaic of broken tiles in the bath, for example.

/ Some assembly is required. Since this style doesn't come neatly boxed, adaptation is essential. Measure items carefully and think about what will be required to make them function in a new way. Four salvaged windows became the doors on two wall cabinets in the kitchen.

/ Find elegance in the mundane. Take a fresh look at functional materials. Tracy likes the sheen and color of copper pipe, so he took advantage of its functional and aesthetic properties when using it in the house.

/ Express deeper meanings. Use materials and furniture that evoke personal feelings. Tracy and Kim chose colors and included pieces that reminded them of events in their lives. The green in the dining room is a color they discussed the first time they met.

/ To have and to hold—for awhile. An eclectic approach readily adapts to change. Colors change, items come and go as personal preferences evolve—and that's OK.

Below Left
Stereo equipment is wired into the end of a wall—readily at hand but not in the way. The rich brown velvet drape is actually the "door" to the bathroom.

Below Center
Glass block brings light from the bathroom window into a dark corner of the dining room. Copper tubing supports glass shelves that display art glass pieces.

Below Right
The downstairs shower is a broken-tile mosaic, similar to the kitchen backsplash. Repeating elements like this throughout the house helps tie the look together.

Above
Curvy, sleek lines of a high-tech sink perfectly complement the soft curves of an Art Deco chest-cum-vanity. A large round mirror visually brings the mosaic across the room.

CREATIVE CLASSIC NOTES

/ A Cottage of Sea and Sky /

| **1900 SQ. FT.** |

When it comes to opening up a small house, white is an excellent beginning or a strong finish, but it is rarely a good solo act. White plays well with others, so give it good company. This philosophy applies to neutrals too: Think of the dullness of having a party with only quiet people of varying shades invited; add a few lively characters, however, and even the wallflowers are drawn into the fun.

To go beyond white, choose one or two colors that express your spirit. Noble, quiet white befriends blue notably well. Add outspoken yellow to the mix for a lively trio. That's what Laura Burrows-Jackson and her husband, Michael Jackson, did at their seaside home. Hues of sea, sun, and sky flow in a way that says this is a place to relax and have fun.

Right
A hanging sign and a console table make a visual wall to define the living room. Light wood floors along with white walls and ceiling keep the space flowing.

Opposite
Look back from the living room: A small sitting-room vignette is framed by French doors. The continuous color scheme allows the two spaces to visually blend.

Taking out the wall to the sunroom created one open, bright room with two functions. Grouping the seating pieces close together around a wood coffee table makes an intimate room-within-a-room.

Reflecting the couple's casual lifestyle, the color scheme connects every space in the house with a sense of ease. Often whimsical, the accessories boldly punctuate the spaces and add to the home's lighthearted feel. As an interior designer, Laura also carefully planned to ensure that new spaces honor the old house while incorporating modern amenities.

/**SIMPLE HARMONY**/ A simple palette of color, thoughtfully used, gives a small house a nice feeling of continuity. But beware, for as straightforward as the look is, varying how the colors are applied is essential: Too much repetition and the look is just plain boring.

/ Refine to define. Use colors that are clearly part of the original palette, but vary the intensity or the dominant color in adjoining spaces to create flow.

/ Pattern the choices. Big and little prints, flowers, stripes, checks, plaids—oh, and solid colors: Use a blend of these to

Opposite
With all the visual geometry going on in this small area—the lines of the beaded board, dropped ceiling, stair rails, window mullions, and door panels—the white walls and ceiling provide the perfect nonplussed backdrop. Wood-toned flooring and rail cap, along with a painted armoire, are defining elements in the space.

Above Left
The color palette is clearly announced in the front entry with a collection of plates. Seashells honor the home's waterfront location. A single deep-color chair with a reed seat, anchors the space and invites guests over the threshold.

Above Right
The painted-on rug that runs along the stairs reflects the colors and patterns of the poster at the landing. It's an effective way to keep the color flowing to the upstairs, and to maintain the whimsical feel every step of the way.

add interest. Be bold and occasionally cross styles too—say, a mod plaid of the palette in a formal room.

/ Embrace diversity. Blend in nonpalette colors with accent items, such as pillows and artwork. Pieces that carry a fleck of the palette or that are in keeping with the style of the room blend in easily.

/ Make accessories work. Lamps and side tables needn't fade into the background. Dress them up in the color palette and give them prominence, accentuating the colors and adding more points of interest.

/ Bigger color, smaller numbers. If you want to keep the look clean and simple, apply color in an inverse relation to the number of items: A lot of items in a room? Keep colors at a minimum.

Below Left
Pine paneling reflects the home's simple roots. Emphasizing blue and white maximizes the serene feeling of the bedroom, a touch of yellow warms. A fluffy comforter, pillows, deep-cushioned chairs, and an ottoman cozy up the space without closing in the walls.

Below Right
Modern luxuries—a big tub and a small deck—are amenable intrusions to the cottage because they're cloaked with key elements (beaded board paneling in the bath, and small scale and simple lines of the deck) that honor the original structure.

Above
In the tiny upstairs guest room, the three-toned palette is replayed in miniature. By honoring the palette, a large modern poster accentuates the space with a twist rather than simply mimicking the style.

NOTEBOOK

/ Color Around the Corner /

Above Left

A consistent color scheme can be used to create harmony in many situations. In the formal living room of an 1100-square-foot home, the boldest color takes the lead on floor and wall, while white tops the space and light blue plays backup.

Left

Sometimes the simplest choices are the most elegant solutions. Draped in neat pleats and an appliquéd motif, the dining-room chairs readily turn the corner for additional seating in the living room.

Above Right

The dining room follows through on the basic color scheme with even more formality but without missing a beat. Take out the leaf and the table goes to round, opening up floor space.

/Design Flash/

An elegant sofa with carved wood detailing and upholstered in simple white does graceful banquette duty. The choice maximizes seating and creates a smooth line on the wall. A très chic choice.

THE SUBTLE TOUCH

/ **Touch and See Duplex** /

1900 SQ. FT. Texture is a visual as well as a tactile element. Incorporated into a room's decoration, it adds depth and interest without dominating or closing in a space. Understanding texture as a visual element takes some practice. Start by looking at the surfaces of the walls, ceiling, and floor. Then visually run a fingertip across the surfaces of everything in a room.

Martha Grimmer uses texture in decorating as readily as paint and textiles. Her talent is her livelihood; she manages an exclusive home furnishings shop. When she bought a bland duplex, she opted for the convenience of a small house knowing that adding texture would add style and interest to flat surfaces.

Right
A gathering of objects on the mantel conveys a sense of the many surfaces: smooth porcelain, rough rusted pots, rounded pillars, votives, and book spines.

Opposite
The living room furnishings are fair-toned and simple, but the room is alive with texture: rough and smooth, thick and thin, deep and shallow, soft and hard.

The resurfacing started with the structure: Concrete floors were scored and stained, ceilings got new rough cedar beams and exterior house siding between the beams, and walls were texturized. The pace kept up as furnishings moved in: A rough-hewn primitive bench in the living room serves as a table; open shelves in the kitchen add depth while stainless-steel appliances, plain cupboards, and concrete countertops smooth the view.

With plenty of contrasting texture, the home's color palette can be simple, even rather subdued, without

Opposite
Texture plays a supporting role on the ceiling of the dining room where a hutch of antiques takes prominence.

Left
The rough-hewn bench is the deepest texture in the living room. Intermediate textures add a dimension of visual interest: exposed beams and siding in the ceiling, thickly plastered walls, smooth velvet curtains, and iron curtain rods and light fixture.

Bottom Left
A dropped ceiling in the kitchen was removed, as was the wall to the dining room, then unpainted, old cedar fencing was installed. A breathably open space resulted.

Lower Right
The most enjoyable layering in this kitchen is the fabric, chicken wire, window pane, and rough pine fronts on the cabinets astride the fridge. They create quite a French country feel.

Opposite
The master bedroom was an attached garage. Old pine doors that grace the wall of closet spaces and an iron plant stand say texture prominently, while the gentle toile fabric of the curtains and chair sits quietly in the background.

Below
Here also, the dropped ceiling was removed, and cedar fencing and beams were added. The built-in bookcases and small table desk evoke a relaxed library feeling.

Right
A dressing table finds the perfect home under a window lost inside a walk-in closet. Recessed ceiling lights ensure consistent lighting.

feeling dull. In this setting, Grimmer's extensive collection of fine antiques gains its due visual prominence.

/ADDING INTEREST/ Diversify your portfolio of textures to liven things up.

/Set a tone. Decide which texture sets the mood; then add contrast. Accent smooth walls and floors with a thick furry rug. Or add a bit of quiet to rough stick furniture with smooth cotton cushions.

/Layer for added effect. Put a mirror in the back of a paneled bookcase, and add an earthen vase in front to create a vignette of textures.

/Include middle ground. Use intermediate textures, say sculpted carpeting and window shutters, to create transitions between extreme textures.

BEING TRUE TO A HUE

/ **High-Note Entertaining** /

1900 SQ. FT. Any small house works best when it has a good job description. Family home, single starter, and such titles are a starting point. Beyond that, personal lifestyle lays the groundwork for decorating choices.

 That's how Linda Westbury decorated her Atlanta cottage. Professionally, she arranges parties for others and speaks on entertaining and decorating. It's debatable whether she takes her work home or takes her home to work. Staying true to classic blue and white makes entertaining a breeze in her small house: Every room feels connected to the others, so guests feel free to move about. Her furnishings, too, can move about because they're related in hue and style.

Right
Even the front of the house displays the homeowner's true colors. The cottage's classic lines and arched facade are perfect for the classic blue and white.

Opposite
Party paraphernalia is at hand for every entertaining opportunity. Well-chosen items make excellent everyday accessories too, so there's no need to hide them away.

74 SMALL HOUSE/BIG STYLE

The Museum of Contemporary Art
Los Angeles
The Panza Collection

aking a house party-friendly requires only a slight shift in decorating approach. After all, a house has to function after the guests leave. **/PARTY ON/** A set color scheme makes selecting items a focused endeavor.

/ Choose what moves. Select items that do multiple duties. Here, duvet covers become tablecloths to cloak the sunroom tables and wicker chairs move easily from room to room because the collection is coordinated.

/ Have on hand. Favorite glassware and serving pieces are on display and ready to go. Also, having candles, napkins, and other party staples at your fingertips makes having an impromptu gathering easy.

/ Repeat for effect. Artful arrangements are attention-getters. Choose a theme—all silver frames or architectural prints—to hold the thought and create gathering points.

Left
A vibrant red rug accents the blue and red accessories in the sitting room. The seating pieces are neutrally toned and the walls a warm white, giving visual elbowroom for the decorative items.

Above
Glorious repetition can be a joy to behold. Generous mats with frames that almost touch make a cozy arrangement. Right angles are softened by the oval frames, urn lamp, and round vase on the side table.

Above
The line between casual and formal fades away in the dining room. Comfortable cane-seat chairs encourage guests to linger. The table setting and classic side table do their jobs with a quiet elegance.

Left
Repetition of another variety appears in the mirrors. Gilt-frame mirrors hung opposite each other infinitely repeat the inviting dinner scene and maximize the feeling of space in the room.

Right
Flower arrangements are a signature of the homeowner's style. She makes vases from any blue or blue-patterned vessel that catches her fancy: glassware, ink bottles, bulb holders, or water bottles.

Above

These wicker chairs mirror each other and reflect blue wicker chairs on the opposite side of the room (see page 75). Wicker is a good choice for entertaining—it's lightweight, making it easy to move to where extra seating is needed.

Right and Far Right

The guest room goes clubhouse casual with plaids and pine. The deep, rich blues create a relaxing, restful feel. In the guest bath, the shower curtain and basin skirt follow the set pattern and color.

Whether you're just moving into a house or updating a home you've lived in for years, sometimes the need for change is compelling. Often, moving in involves a wholesale redo of every room, while changing an existing residence is a job of

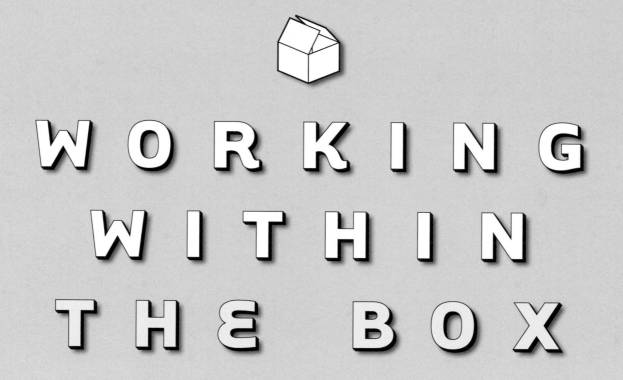

WORKING WITHIN THE BOX

rearranging and updating things. Start by looking beyond what lies in sight to create a vision of what lies ahead. Follow the path of these homeowners to help guide your own steps to updating a home.

SIMPLY MAD FOR TRAD

/ **Suburban Style** /

2000 SQ. FT.

Red brick ranch houses may conjure up the image of a classic suburban home, but they generally don't conjure up an image of high style. Their simple lines, however, don't compete with most types of decor, so these homes of a straightforward design are the perfect backdrop for just about any decorating choice. Interior designer Diane Walton's personal style runs to classic, and she knew the plain rooms of her new house in the 'burbs of Kansas City were just the place to express that style.

The house was standard-issue 1950s, but Walton saw past the the home's past. Knotty-pine paneling and a nondescript fireplace in the family room didn't discourage her. Boring beige tile covering the floors and walls in the bath didn't deter her. In the plain features of the living and dining rooms she saw a blank canvas. With mostly paint and furnishings, the house became an homage to comfortable, traditional style. Not surprisingly, a minor remodeling was required to bring the fifties floor plan to current standards.

Above
Although not a gardener, the homeowner realized that creating a welcoming entry adds appeal. Straightforward landscaping and an elegant bench charm the exterior.

Opposite
Even the entryway has panache. Bold stripes of deep taupe and bright white keep the ceiling up where it belongs and set the tone for the rest of the house.

Removing the wall between the kitchen and family room, and adding style were Walton's priorities. A new, white kitchen with a center island took the place of a dark, closed-off cooking area; the back door moved about a foot into the family room to accommodate the changes. Wood floors got new life with refinishing and careful replacement; new pieces of flooring were alternated with old to blend in. Deep and detailed molding turned an oversize brick hearth into an elegantly appointed fireplace. New white tiles now grace

Left / Before

The wall and change of flooring conspire to shrink the apparent size of both rooms. And the door is practically stuffed in the corner. The brick fireplace is cozy gone awry—too big and simply too flat, making it feel oversized and uninteresting.

Above / After

With the wall out and the wood flooring running continuously through the two rooms, the spaces connect. An area rug with plenty of cozy seating invites lingering in the family room. Note how the pendent light fixtures and work island visually separate the spaces in the gentlest way.

Above / Before

Plain white walls and a continuous run of neutral-colored carpet accentuate the generous size of the living room and dining area but do nothing for creating style. A dark door to the kitchen effectively separates the rooms but looks like a dark splotch on the wall. The ceiling light fixture looks too small for the space.

This Page / After

The best of both: A rug defines the living room, while furnishings and flooring nicely blend the spaces. Bold patterns and tall pieces in the dining room visually enlarge the space.

/Design Flash/

A new pocket door discreetly closes off the kitchen when needed without stealing floor space or attention.

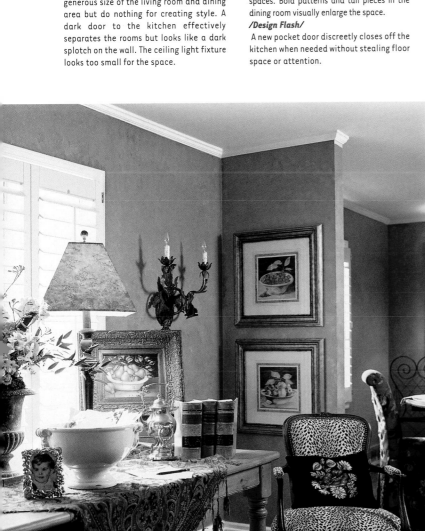

Below / Before
Plain vanilla, the second bedroom was just a box with with windows on the eastern and southern walls.

Bottom / After
Now a home office, the lighting is perfect. Morning and afternoon sun occasionally need moderating; plantation shutters do the job subtly. Putting a large folding screen in the corner reshapes the room and adds focus and a backdrop for the desk.

Below / Before
An exercise in repetition, the bathroom originally sported the same small tile throughout; the floor tile was simply laid on the diagonal.

Bottom / After
Boring no more, the revived bath is decked out in the classic blend of toile and check in black and white. Eight-inch square tiles line only the tub, a quiet choice to contrast to the lively decor.

Below / Before
The master bedroom was free of problems but also unencumbered by any style, a wood floor being the only attractive feature.

Opposite / After
Count the elements of style: Deeply hued walls, restful artwork, cozy sitting/reading space, thick and inviting bedding, generously sized bed, elegant carved side table, white molding and ceiling to punctuate the space—cozy style is layered throughout.

the main bathroom. The rest of the transformation is the result of good decorating. Really.

/GOING GRAND/ Lacking ballroom-size spaces and nosebleed-high ceilings, many suburban small houses require a calculated approach to decorating with classic furnishings. Done with care, this style won't put a chokehold on breathing room.

/Evaluate and prep. Measure rooms, decide what remodeling (if any) needs to be done, and then look at furnishings. Walton's good groundwork gave her an understanding of what would and wouldn't fit in the space.

/Flow forth. Coordinating colors throughout the house makes the spaces visually flow. It establishes a good balance: Spaces are defined but still clearly connected—and, when needed, pieces can move from room to room.

/Go bold one piece at a time. Here, the living room has a generous farm table, the dining room a good-sized server, and a fireplace dominates the family room. The other pieces in each room—the high-back chairs flanking the fireplace, for example—"acknowledge" those pieces without fading to the background. Anchoring rooms with a large piece and complementing it with smaller pieces conveys a feeling of substance without overstuffing.

/Combine highs and lows. Typical of a suburban ranch, the ceiling height here is unvarying at 8 feet. Varying floor, wall, and window treatments create an illusion of changing height. Also, a combination of short and tall decorative pieces gives the eye a chance to move up and down.

Below Left
The picture lamp does double duty, lighting the wall as well as the artwork. Otherwise, two pools of light from lamps at either end of the sofa would leave a dark spot in the middle of the wall.

Below Right
Deep tones in the dining room are warmly lit by a pair of tall lamps. The lamps' dark shades are perfectly apropos for the setting but reduce light output. But the luminosity gets multiplied by the reflective surfaces of the tea and coffee service and mirror.

Opposite Left
A wall between the doors to the bedrooms could be just a blank spot. Instead, Walton created a vignette by continuing the hallway stripes and adding a small chest and picture. A small lamp frames the space with light and gently lights the doorways.

Opposite Right
A masterpiece of lights and mirrors, the generous bathroom mirror has a rich gold frame. Cutting a hole in the mirror allowed the lamp to be set at the right height for casting favorable light on the room and on anyone checking their smile in the mirror.

/ Reflective Qualities /

Making space work is part illusion, and lights and mirrors are two key tools of the illusion trade.

In small houses, the use of light ensures that the walls are extended to their full distance: A shadowy wall or dark corner makes a room seem to stop short. Even a small light moves the wall out to its rightful place, doubly so in a shadowy corner. Lights shining on high keep the ceiling from feeling too close.

Mirrors expand space. A mirror on a dining-room wall reflects across, making the room look twice as big. Framed, picture-size mirrors project the illusion of a window to a space beyond.

Combine lights and mirrors for multiple effects. Look for this savvy illusion in several places in this house: The wattage in the dark entryway gets pumped up by the tall lamp in front of the mirror; the dining-room wall moves back a few feet, and the light is maximum bright without high-wattage bulbs.

A word of caution about mirrors: Check what they reflect. Stand in the mirror's place and look around; avoid creating a view straight into a bathroom or bedroom. To prevent startling people as they walk by, tilt the mirror slightly up or down to change the perspective, and put a tall plant in front of it so the reflection isn't only of ceiling or floor.

LEADER OF THE EVOLUTION

/ A Tale of Then and Now /

1200 SQ. FT. Time doesn't stand still, nor does style. So the house that was sheer perfection 10 years ago may now feel transparently dated. Some homeowners are invigorated by the opportunity for change. Becky Jerdee and her husband, Allen, are just such people. Style maven Becky creates the plan and chooses the furnishings; Allen takes up hammer and saw to give her ideas three dimensions.

For the past 15 years, their creative expression has been wrapped in an unassuming green ranch house. When they moved in—having moved from a large Victorian house in a rural setting—their two children still lived at home, and the flavor was Scandinavian country. In a flourish of fancy, Becky installed a fireplace mantel and an antique door on what was a blank living room wall. Simple, practical bookcases flanked the faux hearth; a bright geometric painting sat in the firebox. Many of the walls were treated to quilt-style murals in soft pastels. As the children left for college, the nest continued its evolution.

Above / Then
A long, blank wall proved the perfect place for folding in the texture of a Victorian home with the smoothness of a tract house.

Opposite / Now
The built-in shelves have been refined, the mantel style simplified with mirrors, and the perfect place for a tête-à-tête added.

Fast forward to today. The built-in cabinets have multiplied to every room, and most of the pastels have faded to white. A short-lived, bright color phase left no trace. The style is serene; stress and tension melt away at the door, and every space functions with the precision of experience.

/STYLE UNBOUND/ Flexing the spaces in a house to adapt to the changing needs of a family requires the shedding of hidebound ideas. /Wait not; want not. Define rooms by function not blueprint, and make those changes when necessary. If, perhaps, you're yearning for a work space but don't have a spare room, look at how you're using rooms and make a plan of adaptation. Here, initially, the parents took the smallest bedroom, their son the "master bedroom," and their college-bound daughter the walk-out basement. The "dining room" has always held a concert-size grand piano. And the "third bedroom" was a dining room that quickly evolved into a workspace. The only changes were the removal of a superfluous half-wall by the front door, the opening up of basement rooms, and the in and out of a decorative door.

Below Left / Then
Subtle pinks defined a quilt pattern on the wall, accenting the stripes in the long, low sofas. The dated picture window hid behind sleek vertical blinds. An indoor Adirondack chair anchored the country-casual feel.

Below Right / Now
A grand piano still stands guard, but the path to the kitchen curves around it now that the Victorian-influence door has been retired. The feeling is even more open and flowing than the original layout.

Opposite / Now
Warm elements—wood tables, sisal rug, and salvaged greenhouse doors—anchor the pale walls and furniture. Matching short sofas flank a bow window that brings in the outdoor view. A whisper of a drape hung on a cable at ceiling height softens the afternoon sun.

Top Left / In Between

Twixt then and now, the Jerdees senior took over the master bedroom, indulging in a queen-size bed and bright colors. But the look remained country with a quilt-influence pattern on the walls, a twig bench at bed's end, and a wicker chair by the window.

Bottom Left / Now

The bow window was such a success in the living room that the Jerdees added one here. The bench at the foot of the bed nods to the Scandinavian influence and provides a place to admire the view when putting on socks and to set clothes.

Below / Now

A built-in headboard frees up floor space. Always wise to the perception of height, Becky kept the vertical stripes that reach almost to the top of the windows; now they're in soft, pale tones. Rather than squeezing in lamps, they opted for wall-mounted lamps that swivel into place for reading.

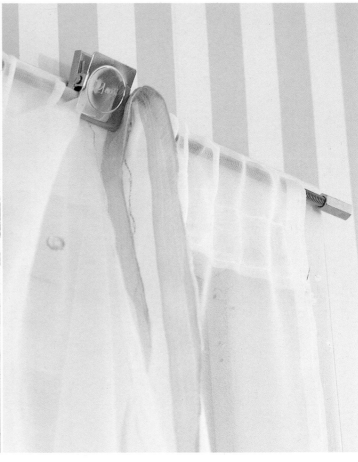

Below Left / Then
When the small bedroom was the master bedroom, the headboard and storage were built in to maximize the space.

Below Right / In Between
When the small bedroom became a guest room, color and graphic accents created a whole different feel—but change required only paint and linens.

Opposite and Above / Now
The guest room now has a subdued tone. Window-high paneling wraps around the room. Repeating the stripes on the cabinet helps incorporate it into the room.

/Design Flash/
Cool accessories needn't be expensive. The drapery hardware is actually threaded rod and clips from a local home center.

/ Please release me. Many family furnishings now grace other homes. When an item's usefulness has expired, it finds a new home. There is little room in a small house for furniture flotsam.

/ Apply a sure hand. Like Fred Astaire and Ginger Rogers dancing, the look of this house seems effortless. In reality, there's a lot of work involved. The Jerdees draw on years of experience to make the changes smooth. If you're unsure about a change, think about how you can do a trial run, perhaps painting only one wall or doing a single room at a time. Changes that don't work can be reworked, and changes that work can be repeated or completed.

Left / Then

Airy and bright, with outdoor furniture doing dining duty, the kitchen had classic appeal. The built-in cabinets added storage; by thoughtfully choosing even the kitchen essentials and exposing the good lines of cookware, these items can be on display in their storage cubbies. Removing doors made the upper cabinets open and airy, too.

Above / Now

Simply a variation on an excellent classic theme, the kitchen now has more warmth with baskets tucked in the cabinet, a wood table, and wicker-seat iron porch chairs. Since dinner for two is now de rigueur, the table was chosen for its fold-away top. Folded up, it's only half the size, freeing up floor space. The cat approves of the choices.

/ Built In to Last /

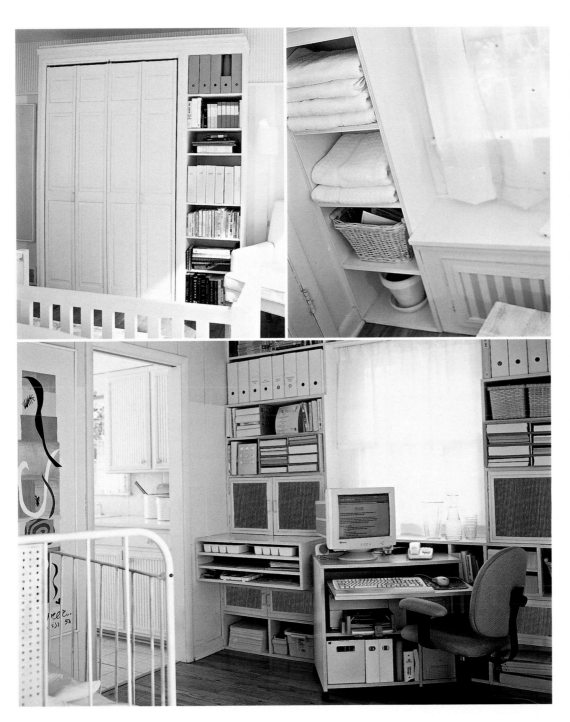

Few would argue the wisdom of adding built-ins to maximize the storage capacity of a small house. But don't stop at simple shelves nor dream wistfully of elegantly appointed cabinetry. The Jerdees built simple cabinets in every room. Paint and a touch of trim make them stylish, but function is the first priority.

In the master bedroom, top left, the cabinet is only a foot deep. Stopping just short of the ceiling, it has the look of a freestanding piece. It adds a tremendous amount of storage but it doesn't interfere with the flow of the room.

Just a touch of storage in the guest room, top right, puts otherwise lost space behind the closet door to good use.

Home offices require plenty of storage. Surrounding the window with shelving, left, and putting the computer on a cart gainfully employs every inch. One of Becky's new trademark sheer curtains keeps glare off the computer screen. Pocket doors at both entrances allow the room to be closed off as needed.

PUT AWAY OR ON DISPLAY

/ The Stuff of Life /

1900 SQ. FT. The amount of stuff one acquires, the saying goes, is equal to the space available—more space, more stuff. However, once the alleged equilibrium is achieved, new stuff still seems to come in while old stuff refuses to budge. Things that have outworn their welcome still occupy space—space that is expensive to own and to maintain. Clearing out and corralling clutter often is referred to as "editing" by people who write about decorating—and clutter control, like the rules of grammar, makes the picture clear.

Left / Before
This is honesty. And, let's be truthful, everyone has had one of those days. Before developing a storage plan, clutter ruled.

Right / After
Anything that does double duty has a place of honor in a small house: The ottoman-coffee table-extra seating-storage cubes get bonus points. Kids and dogs each have one; the third holds blankets and pillows.

A new faux fireplace gives the room a strong focal point, an area rug anchors the furniture, and simpler window treatments quiet the look. Yes, two children, two dogs, and a cat still run madly through this room, but now they have a clear path.

Above / Before
This family engaged in the all-American pastime of horizontal filing in the dining room. It would take half a day just to get the room ready for entertaining guests.

Above Right / After
Relieving the room of dropbox duty brought out the elegant spirit of the dining room. Two upholstered chairs from the living room found a new home here. And the buffet is two wire basket storage pieces with a white top and sleek fabric wrap.

Bottom Left
Once thick with furniture, this area was cleared and put to a new use. The desk moved here from across the room, and a small table that was a too-small nightstand came downstairs to do end table duty by a comfy reading chair.

Bottom Center and Right
A single three-section bookcase holds books that were scattered about the house. Photographs and magazines are neatly boxed and labeled for ready access. The central space was reserved for display.

Above / Before
This elegant piece was lost under an extensive collection of good serving pieces. And the display space lost its focus as well. There was simply no guidance for the eye, not to mention the difficulty in finding a particular piece when it was needed.

Above Right / After
The sideboard's sleek lines are now apparent. Most items are relegated to a cabinet, where they can be readily retrieved and enjoyed on demand. Hanging the artwork from a set height means pieces can be rotated without knocking new holes in the wall.

This is the story of organizing the bustling Hopkins family: two adults, two kids, two dogs, and one very harried cat. Their good taste was evident—perhaps a little too evident—in their stuff. To tame the clutter, they got professional help. The *Better Homes and Gardens*® magazine design squad wrangled the Hopkinses' stuff into elegant submission, giving their style space to shine. Peace now reigns over the household, except for the outnumbered cat.

/STORAGE 101/ Storage has two options—on display or put away. And it has a decorative influence; significant thought is put into pieces that simply hold stuff. Balancing capacity and style is key to organization.

/Remove the glue. Many items develop a thick coat of psychological glue that holds them in place. Look at things objectively and then give some stuff its freedom. Sort out things that can be discarded, given away, or sold. The Hopkinses used the proceeds from a garage sale to buy better storage pieces. Send what's too precious to sell but can't be used currently to out-of-sight storage. This family put some items into storage and others on loan.

/Move it around. Furniture also develops psychological glue. Once a piece of furniture or any other item enters a room, it tends to stay there. Moving things to another room or within a room lightens the load in heavily used areas like living rooms.

Opposite Top Right / Before
This is the master bedroom, but the daughters' stuff and items in transit pretty much commandeered every square inch. Two small nightstands and a closet of meager proportions added to the look of free-floating stuff.

Below / After
Enough space wasn't the problem; it's how space is allocated. The Hopkins chose to add a freestanding "closet." Wire storage pieces are safely anchored to the wall, a ceiling-hung curtain wraps the space. Now there's enough room for a cozy rocking love seat.

Top Left / After
Favorite items and a display cabinet are regrouped and arranged in a place where they can be enjoyed.

Bottom Right / After
Photos have a dedicated place in the display ledge that wraps around three-fourths of the room. A new storage chest at bed's end holds clothes; a bed skirt hides pullout drawers. All this organization, plus new curtains, gives the bed its due focus.

/Designate display. Clear the view by displaying favorite items in certain places. If your collection is large, try rotating displays rather than having everything out all the time.

/Blend in storage. Plastic boxes are effective storage but they lack panache. Invest in some storage choices that fit in stylishly. The new living room bookcases are, well, cases in point. Every piece need not be an heirloom—the freestanding closet in the master bedroom shows the effect of a little ingenuity and a lot of flair.

/Chasten paper. This family tamed the paper tiger: Now they check paper at the door in a catchall back closet, so the stuff never penetrates the living area. The closet is organized to make sorting and disposal painless.

ELEGANT SOLUTIONS

/ Chef's Choice /

520 SQ. FT.

Small houses can have a maddening lack of "black hole" space, whole rooms where items unneeded in the moment can be stashed. Rather, these houses offer up tiny treasures of space that create storage and display with at-your-fingertips access.

Michael Pelkey, chef and dedicated collector, bought a house that can only be described as tiny. It's a former cigar maker's cottage in Key West's historic Old Town district. Restoration guidelines dictated that he could neither change the historic exterior nor add on. The interior, however, was his to do with as he pleased. Which was good because there really wasn't an interior left to the place. Rotting floors, no water or electricity, and plenty of resident insects summed up the home's condition on Pelkey's first visit. But he saw charm and potential—and his brother, a master carpenter, was available to help bring back the charm and realize the potential.

Below
The dining area has a bistro feel with small round tables and window seats. For larger groups, Pelkey put a table for 14 on the deck. Warm yellow paint, rich wood floors, and copper cookware on display create a cozy feeling in this open space.

Opposite
Only the columns and tin roof are original to the house; the rest of the exterior was replaced in period style to meet the community's strict historic guidelines.

Above
Much of the freestanding furniture is in the
living room. Chief among them, high-backed
and covered in a plush fabric, the sofa takes
the attention. Hidden inside the trunk are
holiday decorations. Leggy iron patio chairs
lightly complement the arrangement.

Left
Beyond his collection of ironstone, Pelkey
has a large selection of cook's wares. Deep
built-in cabinets frame the windows and
create the necessary storage for the items.

Opposite Top
Shallow shelves hold Pelkey's extensive
collection of ironstone pudding molds. Rope
molding trims the shelves. It's a simple,
elegant display space with a minimum of
ornamentation. Under the window, a
cabinet hides the television's "black hole"
when not in use.

Opposite Bottom
The fridge is wrapped in storage. Serving
platters slot into cubbies up top and a wine
rack runs down the side. Additional white
ceramic pieces accent the look.

P roviding a secure shell for the interior made restoring the exterior the top priority. That accomplished, Pelkey and his brother removed the remnants of the interior, installing salvaged materials (the windows and flooring), and building in function and style all the way up the walls. Precious floor space opened up by building in all of the lighting, most of the seating, and plenty of storage. Visual bumps were removed: Light switches are placed out of sight, and window and cabinet door latches are discreetly built in. The colors are soft and the fabric patterns subtle. Taking a cue from his extensive ironware collection, Pelkey created a house that's simple, country-inspired, and has elegant lines.

/SMALL MIRACLES/ Getting a full life into 500 square feet requires a big-picture plan and attention to detail.

/Splurge specifically. To stretch a tight budget, indulge carefully. Here, using stock millwork and plain tile cut costs to allow for expensive tile trim on the range hood.

/Deceive with good looks. Cabinet fronts flanking the sink hide the dishwasher and microwave oven. Paneled cabinets in the dining area house cleaning supplies, cookbooks, and a generous supply of dishes.

/Accentuate the positive. Floor-to-ceiling open shelves in the living room display an extensive and beloved collection of ironstone.

/Seek out every niche. Window seats have storage below. The platform bed lifts up to reveal storage. Even the space between the studs in the closet walls works; Pelkey's compact disc collection is tucked in.

/Everything for a reason. All this effort makes the tiny house feel open by keeping the visual surface smooth.

/Design Flash/
Through much of this small house, there's molding at the top of every wall, creating a strong horizontal line at that point. This element both anchors the rooms and lets the beaded board ceiling soar above.

Below Left
Really no more than a room, a guesthouse sits at the back of the deck. High arched windows bring in light while protecting privacy. Built-in bookcases frame a peek-a-boo leaded glass window. The platform bed has storage underneath.

Below Right
What looks like a cabinet next to the sink is actually a facade for the dishwasher. Custom-made iron pins eliminate the need for door pulls that would fussy up the look.

Opposite / Top Right
Everything sits readily at hand in the kitchen. Spices line the shelf behind the generous farm sink. Fabrics with a French provincial feel dress up the glass cabinets and skirt the sink. The necessary light comes from pendent lamps.

Below Left

Even the bed does double duty. The platform is hinged for access to storage below. The bedroom is pretty visible, but a tapestry-style fitted cover and pillows create a daybed look. With the wall lamps, this is a great place to read a book.

Below Right

Putting the porcelain sink on the countertop maximizes precious storage space under the sink. Soaps and sundries sit at hand on the tile shelf. The rounded arch on the fancy mirror adds a soft touch. For privacy, lightweight drapes hang on an iron rod.

The stretching and tweaking of space steps up a notch when the interior of a house is remodeled. The best way to make sure things fall into place when the dust settles is to start the project with a reason, be it better space allocation, improved traffic

SMART REMODELING

flow, a bigger kitchen—whatever suits the needs of you and your family. Think about style as you develop plans and make choices. That's what these homeowners did, and the effort made their homes look wonderful and function fabulously.

CHARACTER REFERENCE

1100 SQ. FT. Few but the dedicated historical renovator buy a house with the intent of restoring it to its original condition. After all, people intend to live their own lives—not the lives of the original owners—in a house. This isn't a hard-line distinction, however. New owners often feel a connection with the people who lived there before: They share a vision of this house as home.

Sometimes the relationship goes further. Kevin Engle's ties to a house near Hollywood, California, are occupational as well as practical. Engle works in feature animation and wanted to buy a reasonably priced house. He got the house Walt Disney lived in at the time Mickey Mouse was created.

The house was a good buy with charming features—diamond-shape windowpanes, arched doorways and ceilings—that made it worth the effort of fixing up. Engle's original plan was straightforward: Fix the cracked foundation, remove old wallpaper, and paint. But the walls held secrets that expanded his plans; the old Disney home became the new Engle remodeling project.

Below
The time-weary exterior got a makeover with a fresh coat of stucco, new shingles, and vintage-style garage doors. Inside, a faux finish on the plain front door and an exotic Moorish wainscoting stencil, *right*, create a 1930s, old-Hollywood feel.

Opposite
A continuation of the wainscoting, along with pooling velvet drapes and a sisal-look rug, gives the dining room the look of an elegant salon. Armchairs and a generously pillowed settee were selected in anticipation of leisurely meals.

When Engle tried to remove the white ceramic tiles covering the living room walls, the plaster came off too. The exposed lath made it clear that the house had no insulation and the plumbing and electrical systems needed replacement. Eventually, he stripped the plaster from all the walls to find out if they were stable. Also, installing insulation and replacing systems is cheaper and easier when the walls are open.

With the home's interior open, Engle was also able to change the floor plan slightly. The kitchen was originally a tangle of three small rooms. Removing a couple of walls and relocating a door created an open, user-friendly kitchen with laundry facilities stacked in a closet.

Keeping the character of the house was important. Engle and designer/builder Robert Young evaluated the home's features one at a time. The hardware on the front door, for example, was sturdy and still functional so the pieces were replated and reinstalled. But the wall-mount sink in the bathroom was ditched in favor of a larger pedestal sink of similar style. Refinishing restored the

Opposite
The 13×20 living room is a step down from the dining room. The vaulted ceiling adds even more height, and the rich, walnut-stained wood floor flows from space to space. This gives the room enough perceived space to comfortably accommodate a generous armoire and a full contingent of well-rounded seating pieces.

Above
Windows flank the fireplace, and a large arched window overlooks the street, providing more than enough light and views. The upholstered screen adds privacy and tones down the sunlight without diminishing the window's visual interest or completely blocking the view.

Opposite

The breakfast nook now opens to the kitchen, allowing sight, light, and plates to flow freely from space to space.

/ Design Flash /

The echo effect—the windows' favored diamond pattern is repeated in the new linoleum floor.

Above

A new gas stove with the look of an antique adds period appeal in the kitchen.

Top Right

Where once there was but a sink and washer is now a full laundry and lots of storage. A larger kitchen, plenty of storage, and convenient cleaning were all accommodated through creatively thinking about space.

Bottom Right

The flowing floor plan makes so much sense, it's hard to imagine that this space was once cut into three small pieces.

elegance of wood floors. The walls? New drywall got a skim coat of plaster to maintain the period look.

/REALISTIC RETRO/ Young refers to this as a "sympathetic renovation." To honor a home's heritage without inhibiting functionality, consider these points:

/ Check the history. If a home is presented as having a pedigree, check it out—especially if the price reflects a premium past. The title lists all past owners. City or county records have that information too.

Above

The chairs speak cozy, the cabinet says dramatic focal point, but the feel is quiet and comfortable because nothing competes. The room has enough furniture and decoration—and smartly stops there.

Opposite Left

The grass-cloth-covered walls and the beaded board ceiling in the bedroom both sit on point. Up on tall legs, a four-poster bed sits lightly. Carved teak furniture with rattan accents exudes a tropical feel.

/BEFORE/

CLOS

BA

MSTR BR
12 X 13

BR
10 X 11

HALL

CLOS

KIT
9 X 8

DINING
12 X 11

LIVING
13 X 20

BRKFST
7 X 7

ENTRY

/AFTER/

MSTR BR
12 X 13

CLOS

BATH

P

W/D

BR
10 X 11

HALL

CLOS

KIT
9 X 15

DINING
12 X 11

LIVING
13 X 20

BRKFST
7 X 7

ENTRY

/ Systems check. Older homes often need new plumbing and wiring, like this one. There's nothing quaint about leaky plumbing. Engle also had to invest in a new sewer and heating and air-conditioning systems. Have a house inspected to get the full picture of its condition.

/ Blend in the modern. Look for ways to fold the new into the old. Here, a new direct-vent gas fireplace was tucked into the existing, but newly tiled, hearth.

/ Accent with details. Look at houses in the neighborhood for ideas. Renovation product catalogs and old photos also offer style clues. Period lighting in the living and dining rooms adds to the old-Hollywood feel of this house.

Top
The new freestanding footed tub and pedestal sink are period perfect. While the design is of the era, the tile is also new. A stained-glass window was designed from a glazed tile from the old fireplace; it allows in light but blocks the view, and sets the bold color scheme.

Above Left
A detail of the headboard shows the intricate wood carving.

Above Right
Rattan and wood details in the bath reflect the style of the bedroom.

BEYOND THE BUNGALOW

1200 SQ. FT. A small house rarely stands alone. Other houses stand all around, and the neighbors may be none too shy in stating their feelings about exterior paint colors, lawn care, and such. In a historic district, the commentary becomes formal and legalized. How a home is shaped beyond the facade, however, is rarely dictated by public policy, allowing for an unfettered expression of personal style regardless of address.

Elizabeth Glassman's dream house was a dilapidated 1920s bungalow with a tiny guesthouse in Santa Fe's historic district. Her taste runs to midcentury modern. Brought in to satisfy both the historic commission's strict aesthetic guidelines and Glassman's personal sensibilities was Carrie Glassman Shoemake, playing the dual (but, thankfully, not dueling) role of architect and sister.

After reviewing several options, the most radical redo was chosen. Like an odd architectural puzzle, the original floor plan squeezed in eight rooms, and the ceiling sat below 8 feet. The resulting airy creation is literally the result of carving out space: The key question was not which walls to remove, but which ones to leave standing.

Below
With the overabundance of walls removed and the ceiling raised to hug the underside of the roof, the house has breathing space in every direction. The neutral, spare backdrop lets Glassman's funky furniture collection take center stage.

The house and guesthouse were each stretched a few feet and now share a wall, but not an entrance. In the main house, the kitchen moved to the front, anchoring the four-space main living area. Living room, kitchen, dining room, and generous entry surround a central fireplace. The neutral white walls and gray concrete floors flow unceasingly, betraying no sense of scale or endpoint. Shoemake's magic with views divides the big room into its four functions. The back of the fireplace defines the entry, drawing a gentle line of privacy from the outside world. The fireplace opening is sharply turned away from the dining room and is only visible from the living room. The kitchen is warmed with alder

Above
Large pieces need their space. Standing guard in the dining room is an imposing red Mennonite armoire. In this open space, the piece has the visual elbowroom it needs.

Opposite
What's not in this abundant space? A single lamp. Windows all around and strategically placed track lights eliminate the need for floor or table lamps and keep the light flowing with the view.

The living room's conversation core is defined by an edged rug and the Rumford fireplace. Each space has a clear focus even though it's open to the others, so the feel is harmonious.

Far Left

For additional storage and work space, an airy central island was included. Visually, this piece continues warming up the feel up the kitchen without obstructing the view.

Left

Not all was tossed out with the walls: Natural wood windows remained and got an update with new hardware. The Arts and Crafts style of large glass panes and simple moldings maintains the required exterior look and is an excellent complement to the straightforward interior.

Opposite

Warm wood tones, strong horizontal lines, and three walls create a cozy wrap for the kitchen space. The high ceiling and absent fourth wall visually attach the kitchen to the rest of the space.

Below

Outdoor views were incorporated at every window. Here the stovetop view is to a new sitting garden where the old driveway ran, and a large window brings the view in all the way from soffit to countertop.

The guesthouse bedroom is a lesson in just enough—just enough color, just enough furnishings, and just enough light to make a stylish and comfortable space with a clear Southwestern flair.

Below

Contrasting before and after floor plans clarify the extent of this remodeling. By staying focused on the homeowner's personal needs and style preferences, the architect created a strikingly clean floor plan from a chaos of rooms. Success like this happens when the architect and homeowner share a vision of the project.

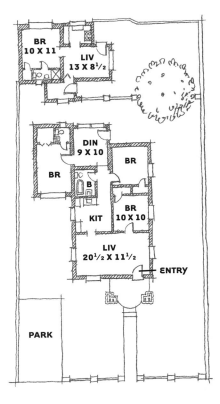

/BEFORE/

/AFTER/

wood cabinets that contrast the cool adjacent spaces. And a large window in the dining room turns the focus to a singular view of a patio.

/**OPENING UP**/ Turning a cluster of rooms into a wide-open space requires more than a sledgehammer:

/Check dem bones. Be sure the structural elements of the house are stable. Professional advice from an architect at the outset helps ensure the integrity of the final design.

/Explore the options. The sisters developed several designs before the work began. By thinking through how each plan would work, the best design evolved.

/Never forget the budget. Once the walls start coming down, a homeowner can get positively giddy with ideas. Everything has a price tag; keep the bottom line in sight.

/Keep options open. Build in flexibility where possible. With a plethora of windows in place but few walls, this house could be readily reconfigured should the need—or desire—arise in the future.

Above
Wall-mounted sinks in all the bathrooms maximize floor space, and niches carved into the walls take the place of shelves that would jut into the airspace.

HINTS OF HISTORY

/ At Home on the Harbor /

1000 SQ. FT.

Two constants prevail in the world of home renovation: The importance of location almost cannot be overstated, and architects adore a challenge. Putting the two elements together can result in a magical creation. A hundred-year-old wreck of a small house with a to-die-for view of the harbor at Marblehead, Massachusetts, was a siren call to architect Bob Zarelli. His wife, Debbie, didn't hear the call, but she appreciated both the home's location and Bob's vision. Game for the adventure, she signed on, and they purchased the house.

The house's shell and mechanical systems were updated posthaste to make the place livable, but the interior creation of Harborwatch, as they call the house, took 12 years. The design anchors on the fine art of space use employed in a ship; the house became Zarelli's laboratory for working with space and fine materials. Removal of most interior walls turned the roughly 400 square feet of the first floor into a single, visually flowing space. Maple flooring runs front to back to maximize the sense of depth, and a mahogany chair rail outlines the space, connecting the rooms and visually widening the narrow house.

Above
For weather fair or foul, hats and coats hold steady at the ready in the mudroom by the side entrance.

Opposite
Double bedecked, the rear of the house has the best views of the waterfront.

mall houses, like ships, have little tolerance for frippery: Most items of beauty must also function. Double decks visually and practically add floor space. Numerous windows bring in light and decorate the walls with the exquisite view. The architect's appreciation of fine materials is especially evident in the choice of black granite for the kitchen and bath countertops. One more wonderful thing about small houses is that expensive materials often can be incorporated because only a relatively small amount is needed.

Upstairs, in a case of adaptive repetition, the elements in the bedroom, study, and bath echo the downstairs design. So, although the spaces aren't connected visually, a sense of continuity is established.

/SHAPING UP/ This house exhibits a mastery of details from many years of effort. The Zarellis took the long view of this project, making choices accordingly.

/Prioritize. Necessity and budget most often determine the order things get done. Here, sealing the exterior from the harsh environment topped the to-do list. Only then could work on the interior proceed.

Opposite
The kitchen has ample space and breathing room but gets the cozy gourmet-galley treatment with a dark soffit to house spotlights; black counters, backsplash, and accents; and warm-toned beech cabinetry that wraps the space.

/ Design Flash /
The molded-glass range hood funnels out cooked air and leaves the view clear.

Right
In a perfect blending of styles old and new, a salvaged mirror and overhead light fixture accent the modern bentwood table and chairs. The crisp lines of the Alvar Aalto reproduction dining furniture play well with the sleek ship detailing of the house.

Above
Optimizing the use of every square foot meant fixing up the real estate down under. Half the cellar is now a study and home to collections of whirligigs, pipes, and travel books.

Left
A bay window brings light and sea views deep into the first floor, and softens the line between indoor and outdoor living spaces. Built-in cabinets create a sense of order and organize books and collectibles.

Right

White paint, wood trim, and a grid of storage mimic the living room design. The custom bed sits high to allow a sea view from a reclining position; the strip of molding visually breaks up the height and offers a step. Skylights bring in the view and prevent the cozy angled ceiling from feeling like a head banger.

Opposite

With the addition of a small custom table, a bedroom becomes a suite. This house takes graciousness a step further with an upper deck.

Below

The generous bathroom mirror reflects the window, light from above, and almost the whole room, creating a sense of spaciousness. The closet doors, reflected in the mirror, are arched like yacht doors.

/ Have the patience of a Cubs' fan. A fixer-upper isn't a good choice for impatient folks with a limited budget. Staying focused on the idyllic setting and what could be helped keep the Zarellis moored through the process and allowed them to enjoy Harborwatch as it evolved.

/ Follow the cues. This house is in Marblehead's historic district, with colonial-style houses all around. Clapboard siding, and interior and exterior moldings nod to the local style. Off-white, exterior-quality fabric for the simple Roman window shades subtly reflects the sails in the harbor. Choices like the shade fabric, that fly just below the radar of recognition, reinforce the ties to place in an understated manner.

/ Adapt and optimize. Dragging a bunch of standard furniture and storage pieces into a small house divvied into three levels borders on the absurd. By forgoing most standard furniture and using well-designed built-ins, space is utilized both practically and aesthetically.

SPLIT-LEVEL SMOOTH

/ In a Plain Brown Wrapper /

| 1750 SQ. FT. | Sometimes a house that is unassuming can be turned into something wonderful. In remodeling, one home may require huge amounts of work—removing walls and changing just about every element—while another has a beauty waiting to be uncovered. Often, it's the beholding eye that determines the route.

The lowly split-level home, for example, has received more than a due share of derision. But look beyond the end of the critic's nose and you may see some wonderful elements, albeit often wrapped in a less-than-appealing package. As they toured a split-level house, Kirk Schlupp and Vicki Semke groaned at the sight of orange and brown shag carpet, dark paneled walls, and heavy, dark drapes. One look up, however, and they knew the house had a lot to offer: a vaulted ceiling of natural-toned Douglas fir, lots of windows, a big yard, and it was only 15 minutes from their Chicago design shop, Mig and Tig. They decided to visually stretch light, height, and sight to the max in order to fit in their taste for bold, sometimes offbeat artwork and generously sized furnishings.

Below
The home's facade is straightforward. The homeowners found no reason to change it; their efforts have been devoted to the living spaces.

Opposite
Removing the wall between dining and living rooms, adding skylights, and painting the walls white created the perfect backdrop for the owners' eclectic art collection.

First out the door was the shag carpet, exposing glorious wood floors beneath. White wood shutters replaced the dreary drapes. And a couple of walls came tumbling down, turning the first floor into one large flowing space. Fortunately, those walls simply divided the space, making removal a messy but relatively uncomplicated choice. Skylights were added to bring natural light all the way from the peak of the roof and deep into the newly opened space.

A second remodeling tackled the upstairs rooms. Enamored with the spacious feeling of the vaulted ceilings downstairs, the couple razed the flat ceiling in the master bedroom. Now, a vaulted white plaster ceiling with skylights pumps up the room's visual volume. New, high ceilings with skylights extend to both upstairs bathrooms, bathing them in natural light. The warm wood flooring, accented with decorative area rugs, and light-reflecting white walls also flow to the upstairs.

/**CLATTER MATTERS**/ Open floor plans assuredly make a small house feel spacious. But taking out the walls removes the sound barriers between rooms. Sound carries far, so people, traffic, pets, whatever, even while out of view, can make their presence known with noise. Here's how to squelch the sound waves.

/ Interior motives. Insulation between *interior* walls and floors is popular in new homes, and might be worth adding when remodeling to restrict noise.

/ Install a door to quiet. Both exterior and interior doors with insulation help absorb sound. New interior doors with lightweight fiberglass or plastic foam insulation will help keep bedrooms and bathrooms quiet.

Opposite
The kitchen sports a new, inviting island and a great view of the outdoors—as well as a view into the fabulous new interior. New stone countertops and backsplash add an elegant touch.

Left
The living room isn't large, but high ceilings, big windows, and the new open floor plan create the feeling of a big space that easily accommodates a large cabinet. Several pieces of artwork, too, are of generous proportion. The homeowners knew that opening up the first floor to its full 750 square feet would give these large-scale creative expressions the room they need.

Right
Sunlight streams in through a wall of glass block and from a skylight. Large stone tile in a neutral color and the pedestal sink make the room look more spacious, and a large mirror reflects views and light.

Opposite
Second hand pieces and fun finds give the guest room a tropical touch anchored by a garage-sale marlin. The elements are arranged to keep the room comfortably cool: The background is neutral and each item has sufficient space.

White walls, high ceilings, and plenty of light give the select, bold art pieces and large furniture the space they need to visually stretch out in the rooms.

/ Hard rocks. Hard surfaces bounce noise exceptionally well; kitchens and bathrooms are notorious for their echoing abilities. Use soft window treatments to absorb noise. Carpet and area rugs help keep footsteps from clattering. Although the original choices in this house weren't very stylish, noise reduction may explain why big, beautiful windows and wood floors went under cover.

It's pretty tough to add sound-absorbing materials in the kitchen, so minimize the amount of noise the room generates. Choose appliances wisely: New low-noise dishwashers help. And use plenty of sound-absorbing textiles in adjacent rooms. In bathrooms, cloth shower curtains and scatter rugs can help immensely.

/ Apply textile style. Hanging a quilt over an open banister or on the wall helps reduce noise in stairways. Upholstered furniture is another good way to muffle musings. The upholstered pieces in this house are sound absorbers, as are the numerous large area rugs.

/ Step on it. Wood flooring can be a bit clattery, but it's usually quieter than tile, concrete, or stone—and it looks warmer, too. Installing a new wood floor is a good time to make a quiet choice; ask about the new noise-reducing materials that can be laid under the flooring to dampen sound.

Below Left
Made of crackled wood and laser-cut steel, the bed makes a grand statement. The curvy headboard is at a good height—not so high that it blocks the window, not so low that it looks stumpy. Simple iron nightstands and elegant lamps flank the bed.

Below Right
Functional but often bland, hallways are the Cinderellas of small houses. Here, wedding photos and an elaborately framed Blue Dog print (a wedding gift) celebrate the couple's nuptial day every day—and turn a blank wall into a mini celebration.

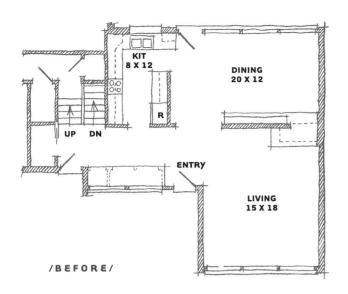

KIT
8 X 12

DINING
20 X 12

R

UP   DN

ENTRY

LIVING
15 X 18

/BEFORE/

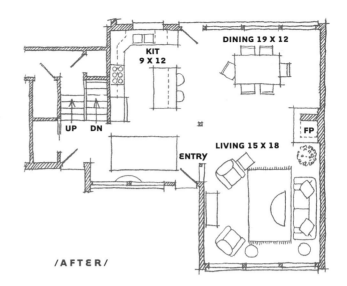

DINING 19 X 12

KIT
9 X 12

FP

UP   DN

LIVING 15 X 18

ENTRY

/AFTER/

Below Left

The effect of skylights is unparalleled, but they can be an expensive option and installation is tricky. Skylights are, basically, windows doing a roof's heavy work. So choose a high-quality window and an expert installer to put in a view of the sky in your house.

/ Design Flash /

Putting lights, like this striking hanging lamp, near skylights creates nighttime light with the same flow as daylight. The lamp also reduces the black hole look large, uncovered windows have at night.

Below Right

A dropped ceiling in the master bedroom became the perfect spot for the television. On a trip, the hotel room the couple stayed in had a TV installed high on the wall, so they took the idea home. Here, it's perfectly placed for watching a movie in bed.

RIGHT SIZE, RIGHT PLACE

/ A Family-Friendly Plan /

| 2000 SQ. FT. |

What kind of house does a successful contractor build? A large house that stands testament to his abilities and achievements? Louis Beacham has been there and done that. However, he and his wife, Debbie, found that living *in* the big house had them living *for* the big house. Upkeep took away from precious time at the beach with their three children, and energy costs were on the rise, pinching the budget for fun. So they cut the square footage in half and multiplied their joy exponentially by refurbishing a vintage bungalow a block from the beach in La Jolla, California.

Since the existing house's only remaining charm was its Arts and Crafts roots (the "room addition" was actually a decrepit trailer parked in back), the Beacham house is an original interpretation that embraces the bungalow and Asian influences often seen in other area homes. For example, bamboo accents the sharp-cornered mission framework in the front gate, an element repeated in the living room ceiling. The result is an organic, airy Zen that accommodates a busy family's needs.

Below / Before
The solid lines of a bungalow-style home are evident in the original house: the long, low horizontal look and low-pitched roof. Clunky siding and shutters, and an overgrown front yard, however, almost obliterated the home's natural charm.

Opposite / After
The bungalow facade was given the full-shingle treatment and a new, covered front porch. The house is on a street busy with beach traffic, but the elegant gate and fence respectfully request that passersby honor this as a private home, please and thank you.

Two layers of tempered glass replace rice paper in the shoji screen. The panels slide shut, blocking out sound but keeping the view to the kitchen and dining room. The concrete hearth wall accentuates the Asian influence to lighten the heavy feeling often found in bungalow-style homes.

Top
Cheery wallpaper and warm wood cabinets and flooring make the kitchen friendly.
/Design Flash / A kid-height fridge built into the big center island keeps snacks both under parental control and within easy reach.

Bottom Left and Right
The living room blends practical and aesthetic. A row of off-the-shelf cabinets contains all of life's clutter with grace, and the ceiling, with rows of bamboo tucked between the beams, is pure style.

Adding a master suite and living room at the back, where the trailer once stood, freed up space at the front of the house. Now the kitchen sits at the center of the home, with a generous center island at the hub of the family's activity. New patios with airy roofs extend the living space front and back.

/GO FIGURE/ Moving a family from a large house to a small one meant getting rid of a lot of stuff, but the Beachams don't miss any of it: They have everything

they need, and now it's all right at hand—including the beach down the block.

/ Good fences, good neighbors. When a house sits on a very public street, a low, stylish fence like the Beachams used is a friendly way to define property lines.

/ Counter culture. Surfaces get a workout in a family home. The Beachams chose concrete and stone for durability and aesthetics. The kitchen counter is a matte-finish granite (easier care than smooth and shiny) and dyed concrete tops bathroom counters. Seashells from family trips were set into the wet concrete, integrating personal treasures in the surface.

/ Configure the house according to needs, not according to tradition. The Beachams' decision to put the dining room where the living room was initially caused some anxiety. But now it feels right because the layout of the entire house works so well.

/ Classic styles unplugged. A heavily style-specific house can feel more like a museum than a home. Good style accommodates variety. The Beachams blended Arts and Crafts with Asian to create a light, bright look that's in keeping with the house's original style.

Above
Concrete floors and countertop are fundamentally durable and uninfluenced by beach sand. Plain-front cabinets and shoji screen closet doors keep the lines simple. Stones become the drawer "hardware," emphasizing the casual feel.

/AFTER/

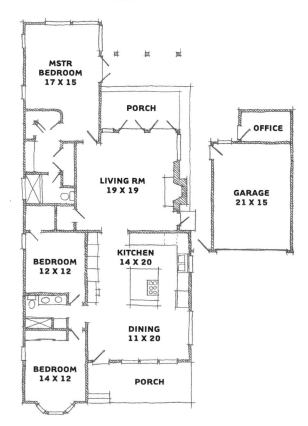

/BEFORE/

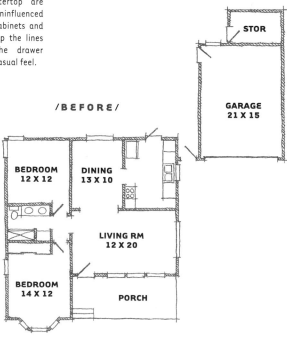

Generous windows and French doors blur the line between indoors and out. Here, the master bedroom's sitting area is actually a covered back patio. The abundance of sunny Southern California days makes outdoor living a year-round joy.

NOTEBOOK

Sufficient bathroom space is a small-house dilemma often solved by remodeling. These examples show how style and elbowroom are just a stroke of creativity away.

Above
A wrap-around vanity makes room for two sinks. The wall-length shower with etched-glass windows and a glass "curtain" gives the big mirrors plenty of light and view to reflect.

Top Right
Keeping enough of an open feel allows cozy details to be incorporated. Here, a pedestal sink keeps space open all the way to the wall, and a skylight opens up the ceiling. The no-door linen closet continues the visual ease. The tub, wrapped in warm-toned tiles and a floral curtain, has a snug feel.

Above and Top Left
The attic suite couldn't hold a regular bath, so the shower, with a skylight, and toilet are tucked under the eaves; the generous dresser-style vanity is in the hall.

Above
The feel is open, the look traditional. The long line of windows above the glass-doored shower brings in light while maintaining privacy.

Eventually the perception of expanded space runs smack into a wall or two. Let's be honest: A 25x40-foot house is a 25x40-foot house evermore, no matter how many visual, storage, and furniture-arranging tricks are employed. To gain more

GAINING SPACE

space, you can use traditional materials and build more rooms, or you can lay claim to some exterior space, weather permitting. And, of course, you can always do a bit of both to get the home that's right for you.

THINGS ARE LOOKING UP

2600 SQ. FT. Creating more living space within a home's existing footprint and under the existing roof is substantially less expensive than building an addition. That's why finishing basements and attics are popular remodeling projects.

Beyond those options, some homes still have places to add space without breaking ground. The direction to look is up: Add a second floor to part of the house. The von Rosenbergs' 1900-square-foot Texas ranch house had little style appeal and a cramped feel. By adding a room over the flat-roofed garage, it now has plenty of elbowroom and style.

To create a cohesive new living space, much of the existing space got rearranged, too. Chopping down a few walls quelled the home's chopped up feeling. The walls of the snug foyer came down, making the front entry area more inviting. Walls that squeezed the kitchen between the living room and dining room came down; a new kitchen twice the size moved in, and the main social spaces moved to the new addition.

Above
One of the few attractive features of this tract house was rough cedar siding. That was a perfect element to carry through to the new garage-top addition.

Opposite
Part of the remodeling plan included the existing house, especially the kitchen. It was a walk-through work space that became an eye-catching hub.

Opposite
One side of the kitchen now opens up to an informal eating area, a perfect place for the homeowners' teenage daughter to host pizza parties. Put to good use, the space below the windows has built-in bookcases to display collectibles and hold cookbooks.

Right
Three tall windows, with a matching set at the other end, bring light deep into the 31-foot-long room without overwhelming the space. Although the generous size of the room could have accommodated a single large window, this arrangement is more in proportion with the existing house. Details like this help keep an addition from looking stuck on and sticking out.

Below
Texas-related collectibles and antiques now have plenty of room to spread out—and to be enjoyed. Making room for favorite things is an important part of successful remodeling.

With careful consideration, the von Rosenbergs were able to minimize some costs. The old roof was trimmed to accommodate the roof of the addition. The siding, an asset on the old house, was extended to wrap the new space. Even the existing kitchen floor, toast-colored Italian tile, fit with the style and layout of the new floor plan. Simple elements connect the spaces: new wood windows trimmed with a bead along the top and a warm-toned color palette.

/BLENDING SPACES/ Adding square footage to an existing house requires a thoughtful blending and defining of spaces old and new.

/Continuity flows of consistency. An abrupt shift in materials sets new spaces apart. Instead, use colors, flooring, and trim in both old and new spaces to blend.

/Open wide and say ahh. Leaving a remnant of the original dividing wall is necessary to signify a change (structurally, it may even have to stay), but wide-open doors help to meld spaces. French doors are great for marking a transition without drawing a hard line.

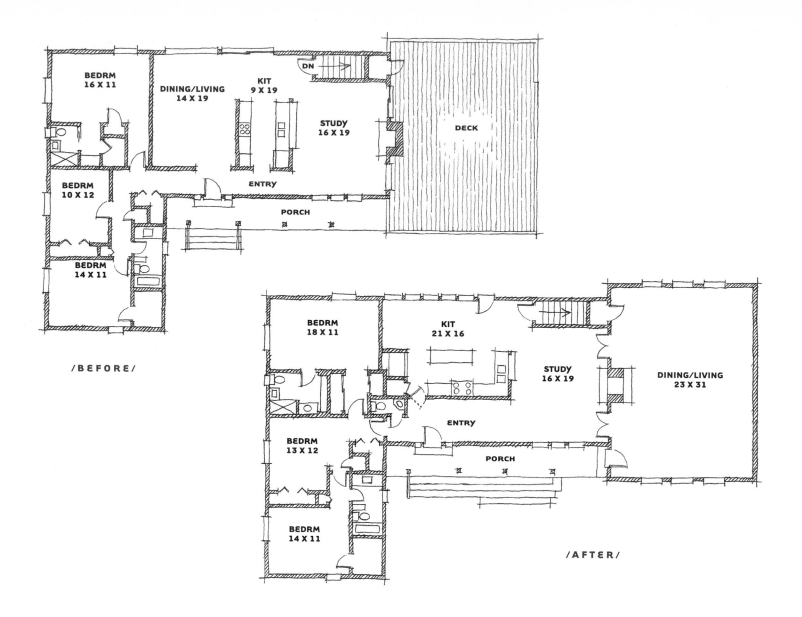

BEDRM
16 X 11

DINING/LIVING
14 X 19

KIT
9 X 19

DN

STUDY
16 X 19

DECK

BEDRM
10 X 12

ENTRY

PORCH

BEDRM
14 X 11

/BEFORE/

BEDRM
18 X 11

KIT
21 X 16

STUDY
16 X 19

DINING/LIVING
23 X 31

BEDRM
13 X 12

ENTRY

PORCH

BEDRM
14 X 11

/AFTER/

/Get on solid ground. The overwhelming openness of an addition, especially a single large room like this one, can make space seem to float. Define the use of each area, create a focal point, and group furniture to guide the eye and foot as people enter the room. In this house, the dining area runs along the front wall and the conversation area is clustered around an area rug.

/A note of caution. While there's something undeniably cathartic about removing an inhibiting wall to open up spaces, first check whether it's doing an important job—holding up your roof. Have an engineer or architect recommend ways to move a supporting wall or reduce its size. Nonsupporting walls? Topple at will!

Left
Exposed beams and a wood ceiling warm the space from above, a feeling reflected in the wood floor.

Opposite
At 700 square feet with a 16-foot-high ceiling, this room could be just a cavernous space. Smart placement of furniture and lighting clearly defines separate areas: Dining area under the hanging lights, and conversation area circling around a rug. A clear path between the two allows traffic from the kitchen and study to enter the room.

TIME AFTER TIME

/ **Stay Put and Branch Out** /

| **2400 SQ. FT.** | A small house occasionally experiences a growth spurt

later in its life. Even when a homeowner's priorities and needs change, ties emotional and budgetary often make staying put the best choice. Fern Smith raised a family in a 1200-square-foot ranch house in Austin, Texas. Bought as a fixer-upper, the house was stripped to the studs to clear out the detritus from years of neglect. Remodeling consisted mostly of system upgrades and cosmetic enhancement. Aside from the tiny kitchen, the floor plan worked, so they decided save up to make substantial changes in two years, making do until then.

   Change, however, didn't come for a decade, when Smith decided to move her thriving interior decorating business from a downtown office into the house. The house almost doubled in size, but the budget allowed for few frills, and the right-sized, expanded house doesn't loom over its neighbors.

Above Left and Right
Situated in the home's original living room, the new dining room has plenty of room for a table full of guests. One of the few luxurious appointments Smith indulged in was this silk Fortuny chandelier.

Opposite
Sleek metal roofing covers the expanded house and extends over a new porch. It's one element used to blend old and new, giving the revived house a cohesive look and feel. The style? The homeowner calls it traditional with a twist.

Extending behind the existing house is a new wing for additional living space, and the new office occupies an additional 700 square feet in a partial second story. The home's front was reconfigured to create a welcoming entry that clearly guides clients to the office, and provides a buffer between business and home space. The kitchen gained only 3 feet of depth, but smart space usage makes it work infinitely better.

Living in a house for years gives one ample opportunity to develop an extensive woulda-shoulda-coulda wish list, especially if, like this homeowner, an earlier partial remodeling left some desires unfulfilled.

/MOVE UP, FIT IN/ Without a solid plan, a major remodeling can be an expensive exercise in frustration. Focus on the desired end result, and keep a close eye on the economic picture.

Below
The family room sits at the crossroads of old and new spaces, but the inviting conversation of furniture makes it a place to linger rather than just pass through. The broad opening to the kitchen clearly divides but keeps the view open.

Right
Designed to conceal the bottom of a stair case, the arch is a charming focal point. And it plays with perspective, visually stretching the kitchen: The arch's extended length makes the room look wider, and the lower end points visually raise the center.

/Respect the neighborhood. Smith was adamant about ensuring that her expanded house fit in the neighborhood in style and size. Most new space is not visible from the street. Aside from aesthetics, keep in mind that the square-foot resale value of an overscaled house is usually lower than that of surrounding houses.

/Watch interior proportions. If tiny rooms have put the squeeze on you, the urge to add gymnasium-size rooms may be overwhelming. For comfort in the long run, fight that urge and keep the rooms in scale with the existing house. Making changes to the rooms adjacent to the new space also helps maintain the flow.

/Carry on. Repeating a simple, understated element subtly pulls spaces together. The reappearing grid in the cabinets of this house isn't obvious, it's a just-under-the-radar consistent feature slipped in at appropriate places.

/Approach alternatives. Be open-minded about savvy choices that achieve a look for less cash. Using less expensive look-alike materials, for example, can save the budget without sacrificing style: Smith wanted marble for the master bath and kitchen. Substituting travertine tile in the bath and glossy white, hand-fired tiles in the kitchen left enough in the budget for a desired full contingent of grade-A kitchen appliances.

Opposite

Bunches of built-ins create an abundance of storage without stealing floor space. The bookcase grid mimics the kitchen cabinetry for a consistent look throughout the house. For a smoother appearance, however, the cabinet doors below are unadorned except for hardware.

Above

Grouping artwork in a small cluster like this creates a scenic vignette. Framed by the window and doorway, the grouping becomes concentrated, undiluted by an excess of space between items.

Above Right

Style opportunities are everywhere. This could have been just a hallway to the master bedroom. Taking advantage of the change in the elevation, the ceiling was kept high and a well-lit gallery space graces the hall. French doors lead out to the backyard.

Right

Details make the master bath. Antique ornate sconces and mirror adorn the wall, and the walls are subtly patterned; the cost-effective tin countertop is the perfect foil to these decorative elements.

Right and Below
Pure glam, a canopy bed in the master bedroom takes advantage of the high ceiling; a wrap of sheer curtains turns it into a cozy island in the clouds. Symmetry in pairs of windows, dressers, and wall-mounted lamps plays up the grandeur. Light, elegant seating choices float at bed's end to complete the picture

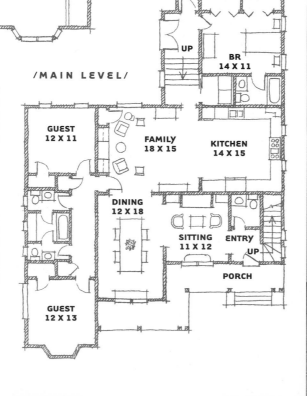

/UPPER LEVEL/

STORAGE 9 X 9

CONFER 9 X 9

DN

OFFICE 14 X 22

STORAGE

CLOS

MSTR BR 18 X 14

UP

BR 14 X 11

/MAIN LEVEL/

Right
The original house ended at the exterior wall of the guest and family rooms. Where the stairs are now is new space all the way back, as is the upper level. Planning made the new house look and feel as though it's always been this way.

GUEST 12 X 11

FAMILY 18 X 15

KITCHEN 14 X 15

DINING 12 X 18

SITTING 11 X 12

ENTRY

UP

Opposite
'Twixt public and private spaces, the small sitting room off the entry emphasizes an intimate feeling with a well-pillowed antique Louis XVI daybed surrounded by cabinetry. The bookcases echo the look of the kitchen cabinets and keep a consistent feel flowing through the house.

GUEST 12 X 13

PORCH

NOTEBOOK

Angling for Successful Remodeling

Remodeling is contagious. These Atlanta homeowners started with a kitchen redo, which, for entertaining purposes, required dressing up the adjacent den. An attic master suite and better outdoor living space round out the picture. The home's footprint, however, didn't change: The gained space (real and perceived) is achieved with a mastery of angles. Increasing the angle of the roof created the master suite from a cramped attic. Downstairs, new angles made existing space work better.

Below left
Do the math: Raising the roof four feet, and adding three windows and two dormers equals a spacious suite from 300 square feet of previously unused attic space.

Below Right
Still square, the den and kitchen now look at each other from an angle created by the new media center. That gives both spaces a more interesting and longer view.

Right
Scaling back a large deck improved the view from the French doors to the wooded backyard. The new deck, tucked in the corner, draws guests farther outside to an inviting terrace just a few steps below.

Below Left
Wine storage and a large refrigerator nest in behind the media center. The new ceiling bows up into empty attic space. It's an eye-catching, space-enhancing detail.

Below Right
Going diagonal greatly increased the kitchen's workable space. A zigzag granite counter winds into space that was a little-used breakfast nook.

NOTEBOOK

Expanding living space to the outdoors makes any small house live well. Climate conditions affect how often you can use the space, but you can always visually bring it inside. Integrating the outdoors and the indoors can be as simple as taking advantage of what nature has provided or as complex as adding a structure. The nature surrounding your house will give you clues.

Getting a feeling of déjà vu? All of the outdoor living spaces collected here are connected to houses featured in this book. But, just like the interiors, no single approach fits all. Enjoy this select group of ideas.

Left
Rural acreage properties sometimes have ponds—ahh, just another reason to move to the country. Nature knows best, so why mess with her perfection? Simply trimming back the weeds and adding a few plants at water's edge framed the view perfectly for this Kansas home. (See page 52.)

Opposite and Above
Tucked in a suburban backyard, this petite structure provides ambience for dining, reading, and relaxing. Like an English folly, it includes all the fine finishing flourishes, but the owners achieved the look at a modest price. It's an extravagance of the heart made to delight eye and soul. (See page 94.)

Top Left
Sometimes the best view of the water is from up high. Enclosing the top of the front bay window with a Chippendale railing turned a flat roof into a private porch for the carriage house. The simple iron table and chairs invite relaxation at the end of the day. (See page 16.)

Top Right
Originally as unprepossessing as the front facade, the backyard of a split-level house came to life with landscaping. Limestone and brick pavers replace bland concrete, and ironwork trellises and railings frame the outdoor room. Summertime finds the space thick with plants. (See page 140.)

Above
Several small patios create enticing vistas outside the windows of this Phoenix bungalow; a larger patio accommodates outdoor entertaining. Shrubs and trees provide shade and add a cool garden feel, and combined with a wood fence, add a note of privacy. (See page 124.)

Building a new small house is headline news because it's a "Man Bites Dog" choice in a marketplace of large-home building. These homeowners dared to build small, and their houses provide refreshing examples of the great spaces that can

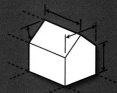

CREATING NEW SPACES

take shape in a small footprint. Like many homeowners, the people who built these homes had budget constraints, so they carefully chose the details that would make their homes function well and live wonderfully.

PEAKED INTEREST

/ **Mountains and Gables** /

2120 SQ. FT. Whether it's a pick-a-floor-plan tract home or a one-of-a-kind custom home, building a new house is an exhilarating experience full of ups and downs. Find the right people to help you, and the process can be a joy.

Judy and Dale Schouweiler live in Colorado but wanted a house of Nantucket style. They found an architect, Elizabeth Waldorf, who appreciated these seemingly conflicting sensibilities, and who could help them create such a home within the framework of a set budget and limited time. The couple collected images of homes they liked and samples of materials they wanted in the house. These items formed the basis of discussions with the architect, who then developed plans for a custom gabled house that's at home in the Western hills.

Right
"Save the trees" was the homeowners' charge. An accommodating deck shows how the character of the deeply wooded lot was maintained. The plethora of gables and windows allow in plenty of sunlight.

Opposite
Repeating rounded arches and peaked ceilings define a room for each function in the long central space. An open community of light and views visually expands the entire area.

Beyond material choices and the appearance of the house, the Schouweilers and Waldorf talked about how the family of four would live in the house—when and where they eat together, what rooms they gather in, what rooms each family member heads to for privacy, and the kinds of entertaining they do. Waldorf also talked to the couple about furnishings and artwork that they would bring to a new house. Places for furniture and favorite artwork were built into the home's plans.

Creating the preferred amount of openness or coziness in the new house was also discussed. The Schouweilers noted that the cottages they liked had a cozy feeling. But looking at the house they built, it's clear they also wanted open spaces. Good communication with the architect prevented disappointment.

The architect found ways to stretch dollars without compromising style. Pine floors are an inexpensive choice that fit perfectly with this home's style. Using standard-size windows and stock cabinetry also helped stretch the budget.

Left
A cheery palette accentuates the bright and airy feel of the design. Gently intersecting the long space is a lower-ceilinged "hall" that guides the traffic.

Above
A bright yellow door provides a lively greeting and a hint of the interior. Though it is attached to the house, the garage clearly stands away from the main structure.

Another set of dueling concerns—keeping as many trees as possible and getting plenty of natural light in the house was resolved with a twofold approach: Careful placement of the house on the site ensured a maximum of both sunlight and trees. And light enters and flows throughout the house by skylights and dormers in the tall ceilings, plenty of windows, glass doors, and interior windows.

/ARCHITECTURAL ENDEAVORS/ Building a new home requires hundreds of decisions. Make the process easier by considering the big-picture issues first.

/ A meeting of the minds. Establishing and maintaining a good rapport with an architect keeps communication smooth. The collaboration here between homeowners and architect was a success because of a shared understanding of what the project entailed.

Above
Separate but joined, the library stays visually connected to the adjacent living room with interior windows and a two-sided fireplace. A single doorway, however, makes it clear that this is a separate and quieter place than the community rooms just beyond.

Right
Pine planks running the length of the main floor tie all the rooms together.

/ **Design Flash** / Including light fixtures and stereo speakers in the building design ensures that they function their best while intruding the least.

/ Identify priorities. Separate the things you want in a new house into two categories: need-to-have and nice-to-have. Items on the Schouweilers' need-to-have list were addressed first and designed in; the budget still had room for a nice-to-have two-sided fireplace.

/ Plan for the future. A bonus room gives you room to adapt rather than move when needs change; the unfinished basement in this house could become a home office or family room whenever necessary. Also, have your architect include wiring for future computer, electrical, and security needs. This is much less expensive to do when a house is being constructed.

/ Consider the site. The ground underneath and around the house often affects how a house is placed. To take advantage of the sloping lot, this house sits on four levels, each just a half-floor up or down from the next.

Opposite
Dormers and sloped ceilings add charm to the house. By incorporating windows, lights, and cabinets into those spaces, the small master bath has all the required elements without feeling cramped. A generous mirror also adapts to the angles and reflects the spacious look and feel.

Above Left
Up a half-story, the master suite gets light, height, and sight from an interior window up top of the door. The closet and bath are closest to the stairs (the doors on either side of the hall); the master bedroom retreats to the end of the hall for privacy.

Above Right
Following the roof's peak, the master bedroom ceiling gains headroom and a spacious feeling. Though tall, the peaked dormers are narrow, adding a cozy feeling. Built-in bookcases needn't be grand: These simple, open bookcases gain interest with the arrangement of tomes and art.

IN KEEPING

1250 SQ. FT.

If you had to rebuild your house right where it stands, what would you change? What would you keep? Although you probably won't experience this situation, considering it is a good exercise for determining what you want and need in a home.

California architect William Glass had a client whose bungalow home had been destroyed in a firestorm; the new home had to be built within the same footprint as the original. Many of the neighbors added a second story, doubling the size of their homes, when they rebuilt, but Glass's client wasn't interested in the added expense of building the additional space. She simply wanted a house that would take advantage of the ridge-top location to provide a great view of San Francisco Bay.

The design of the new house is quite a departure from the original no-character, cramped bungalow. A trace of New England saltbox style shows in the home's gabled roof. And the interior was completely reconfigured to a flowing, open floor plan.

Above
With white trim punctuating windows and doors, the exterior style is as clean as the interior. Although unlike its neighbors, the house is simple enough to blend in nicely.

Opposite
A strip of wall at the ceiling separates kitchen and dining room; it hooks up with a partial wall separating kitchen and entry. White light fixtures blend into the walls.

Using good materials and thoughtful design can make a home's basic elements a focal point. The intersecting lines of the exposed beams, rafters, and trusses, walls, and built-in cabinetry create a flowing, elegant geometry. Indirect lighting is tucked in the partition walls to illuminate the ceiling at night.

oaring, exposed Douglas fir beam, truss and rafter ceilings, lots of windows, and an airy, open floor plan define the new house. The living and dining rooms and kitchen create a single flowing space that makes the house perfect for entertaining. A peaked-ceiling corridor runs the width of the house, lightly but clearly dividing living and dining rooms; narrowing at the far side, it also clearly denotes the home's private space: two bedrooms and baths.

The home's simple forms and natural materials give it interest without ostentation: Generous use of rich, natural wood for the floors as well as the ceiling eliminates the need for additional ornamentation.

A balcony on the front and a generous patio in the back provide easily accessible outdoor living space.

Left
A continuous skylight runs the full length of the ridge forming the central corridor.

Below Left
Horizontal elements—the light fixtures, crossbraces, top of the French doors, and lower sidewalls—create a visual ceiling line in the dining area.

Below Right
A large single-pane window in the master bedroom lets in light and views of the hallway and ceiling of the other bedroom.

/Design Flash/
Flat doors and plain molding painted white disappear into the wall and keep the view clean and smooth.

/FLOOR PLAN TIPS/ The edict of every small-house floor plan is waste not floor space. Think about everything that takes up floor space and how these items can be moved or removed.

/ Eliminate long hallways. A short hallway with a hub of doorways at the end gives each room a few extra square feet. The corridor to the bedrooms in this house is brief, and it's open to the far wall for stairs to a tucked-under garage and two storage rooms.

/ Shrink the entry spaces. A small space is all that's needed to get people in and out of the house, and to collect coats and belongings.

/ Build-in and blend. The small house perennial favorite, built-in cabinets, allows for storage, display, and, in this house, an architectural focal point.

/ Create the short divide. Not every wall can be removed, but many can be scaled down. Low walls open up the view from room to room. Knee walls effectively and safely border stairs and loft spaces, and a wall of low cabinets between the kitchen and dining room, as in this house, can provide needed storage and counter space.

Above
Retaining walls and fill create a small yard on top of the ridge. French doors to the dining room and kitchen make the patio a favorite spot for alfresco dining.

Opposite
Sleek and solid, the granite fireplace didn't need to be fancy to gain focal point status. Also sleek in design, the built-in bookshelves flanking the fireplace provide plenty of room for displaying artwork.

MATERIAL MAGIC

/ Beauty and the Budget /

1200 SQ. FT. Creative solutions are often viewed as sudden events, but in reality, an Aha! moment is more likely the result of hard work than a freestanding flash of inspiration. So, the houses that wow are likely to come from a mind with experience working with the elements of building.

Expertise, however, isn't the only resource for creating inspired homes. Determined homeowners can turn their personal skills into building skills. Nancy and Dennis Biasi worked with patience and ingenuity to create a stunning riverfront home near Mount Hood, Oregon. It all started with a smart buy on a heavily wooded lot on the river. All they had to do was clear away the debris on the lot, which included the remnants of an old cabin that had burned down.

Right
Visitors are introduced to the Biasis' skills at the door: The bench is from salvaged wood and the door is a half-price buy. The door's steel straps were found on the property.

Opposite
An artful arrangement of windows brings sunlight and river views deep into the house. Configuring standard units cost substantially less than using custom windows.

The couple and their two sons made the design and building of the house a family adventure. The longest, most arduous chore was two years spent clearing the land. The job, however, had benefits: Wood and miscellaneous pieces of hardware were salvaged for reuse, and vehicles abandoned on the site were sold for scrap. The Biasis also developed a sense of the site and knew where to position windows to take best advantage of the view and sunlight.

The old cabin's foundation, undamaged by the fire, became the basis for the new house. The Biasis developed the home's design themselves, hiring a builder friend for advice. The couple also smartly realized they couldn't do everything; they hired a framer and plumber and got professional guidance on other areas of construction.

Inveterate bargain-hunters, the couple used second-hand cabinets, tile seconds and odd lots, and doors from a salvage supply house to keep costs low. One savings was accidental: A kitchen island was planned, but the farm table did the job so well, an island seemed superfluous.

/SWEAT EQUITY/ Using the hands-on, low-dollar approach to home construction is likely to be a

Vaulting part of the ceiling brings light and views from the southern windows into both floors and makes the small family room look much larger. Sconces maximize the feeling of height at night.

Storage in the sleeping loft is a funky mishmash of cabinets, painted purple for a punch of color. Exposed collar ties with recessed lighting maximize the feeling of height on the second floor.

long-term investment of personal time and elbow grease. This house was four years in the making.

/ Thrill at the hunt. Watch for sales; go to salvage shops or any place that sells home building and decorating materials at a discount. These homeowners frequented damaged-freight stores, buying everything from wiring to building materials there.

/ Study up. Read up on the work you intend to do, and talk to people you trust for advice. Also, find out the building codes in your area. Certain kinds of work can only be done by licensed professionals.

/ Trade out. Not every transaction needs to be in cash. Consider exchanging your time and talents for products or services. Dennis Biasi's design and advertising skills were the currency for the tile that fills the house.

/ Simplify. A square or near square foundation, a minimum of details, and an open floor plan are cost-effective, and they make building easier and faster. Add only the embellishments—intricate moldings, bay windows, multiple bathrooms—that will optimize the livability of the house. A kitchen bump-out and a sink in the sleeping loft are the only extras in the Biasi house.

Below Left
Open to the living area, the sleeping loft takes in views of the living room, the trees, and the river beyond. In addition to the two bedrooms upstairs, there is a guest room/den on the first floor.

Below Right
For convenience, a sink and mirror were built into the sleeping loft. The Biasis' scrounging and bartering skills created this eclectic collection of tiles and cabinets; since nothing matches, nothing looks out of place.

Opposite Right
Every item in the bathroom was bought at substantial discount. By going to secondhand and damaged-freight shops regularly, the homeowners got the right pieces. The mosaic effect of the tile plays up the eclectic feel.

Below Left
An extra bed for extra company sits at the entry of the large sleeping loft. While not overly private, this option plays up the weekend-home feel of the house.

Below Right
Bought from a company that recycles building materials, all the doors are different. This whimsical choice graces a closet in the sleeping loft.

Furniture placement often falls to the extremes: The Lineup, where every piece stands back firmly planted against the wall—as though one piece has committed a crime—and The Obstacle Course, where every piece floats in a free-flowing

FURNITURE AND ARRANGING

montage and negotiating a path through the arrangement could be a timed event worthy of a medal. Balance is best; this section gives you an overview of how to choose and place furniture to create that blissful balance.

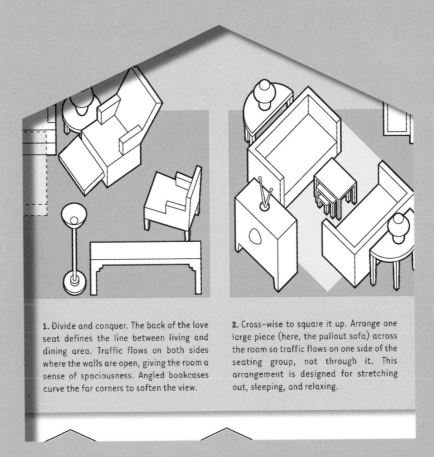

1. Divide and conquer. The back of the love seat defines the line between living and dining area. Traffic flows on both sides where the walls are open, giving the room a sense of spaciousness. Angled bookcases curve the far corners to soften the view.

2. Cross-wise to square it up. Arrange one large piece (here, the pullout sofa) across the room so traffic flows on one side of the seating group, not through it. This arrangement is designed for stretching out, sleeping, and relaxing.

/THE CORRIDOR ROOM/

Typical of tract homes, the corridor living room connects the front entry with the rest of the house. Here, the front entry is at the lower left corner. The entry to the kitchen is straight across the space. Kitty-corner to the entry is a hallway to the bedrooms. Clearly directing foot traffic through the space is the main concern. Arrange furniture so traffic flows around—not through—the conversation area. Avoid placing too many pieces along the walls because that encourages people to walk through the open spaces between the chairs and sofa. Group the seating pieces together to guide people to walk behind or beside the furniture, not between pieces.

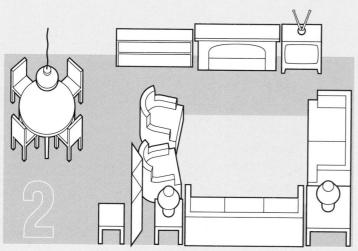

1. A dining area is incorporated in the living room to create an open entry with room for bookshelves. Grouped for conversation, the sofa, love seat, and dining table chairs cluster around an area rug. Traffic flows along a gallery wall to the hallway.

2. With a round table to open up the space, the dining area nests on one side. The conversation area is clearly separate, open to a fireplace and the television along the wall. A folding screen and catch-all end table define the entry space.

3. With the eating area moved to the kitchen, room for a piano moves in. Angling the piano and small sofas increases the sense of spaciousness. A small table and chairs by the fire are perfect when dinner is for two or for reading the mail.

12 SMART FURNITURE CHOICES

Choosing the right pieces of furniture is often an angst-inducing experience. There are so many choices—and options for each choice. Function, of course, is the first and foremost determining factor, small space decorating requires that many pieces perform more than one task and size is always a concern: Like Goldilocks choosing a chair, the goal is to get everything just right. Here are a dozen furniture choices that work well in small houses. Look for them in the style of decorating that best suits your preference, and don't hesitate to mix and match until you find a combination that works for you.

/THE TUNNEL ROOM/

Living rooms and family rooms with a single entrance are apt to appear overly long and narrow. Change the look to wide and spacious by breaking up the view with furniture. Pieces placed at an angle, tables with curves, or couches set crosswise in the room are options for broadening the look and feel of a room—and for getting one space to serve two purposes. These arrangements also direct traffic gently around the conversation area rather than in a beeline toward the far wall. Think first of how you'll use the room; then move on to choosing and placing the right pieces for the job.

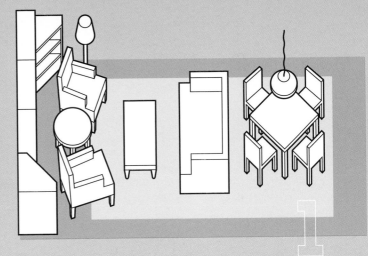

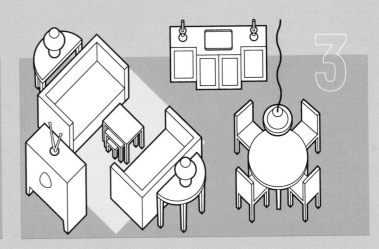

1. Divide and conquer. The back of the love seat defines the line between living and dining areas. Traffic flows on both sides where the walls are open, giving the room a sense of spaciousness. Angled bookcases curve the far corners to soften the view.

2. Cross-wise to square it up. Arrange one large piece (here, the pullout sofa) across the room so traffic flows on one side of the seating group, not through it. This arrangement is designed for stretching out, sleeping, and relaxing.

3. Try another angle—diagonal. The tried-and-true diagonal play is sure to free up a long, dull, narrow space and turn it into an open active area. To really play up the angle, lay tile on the diagonal.

MODULAR SHELVING AND BOOKCASES

These pieces are standard issue for every home. Bookcases and shelving units don't just serve as places to put stuff, they can become focal points in a room, a visual reference to how the room live and works. Decide whether the stuff you stash should be seen or hidden, at hand or behind doors. Then determine if the cabinets should be built in or free-floating, and mix and match from the options available.

/Design Flash/

These pieces run in packs. Cluster cases for maximum storage, or put them back to back to divide spaces.

/THE L-SHAPE ROOM - A Series/

In the 1970s, homes in building developments often sported an L-shape room. The short end of the arrangement is generally labeled "dining area" on the floor plan; the rest of the space is the living room or family room, where several uses often can be accommodated. While the open space of this type of room is a plus, it can look too busy if a lot of small-scale pieces fill the room, and the traffic flow can be clumsy. Of course, you needn't define the space strictly according to the builder's floor plan. Decide where you'd like to dine and where to relax. Then wisely choose several pieces to serve your purposes.

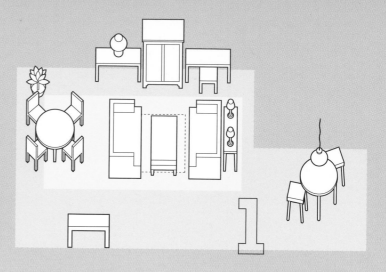

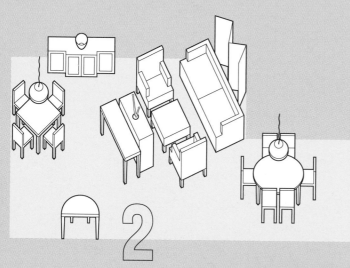

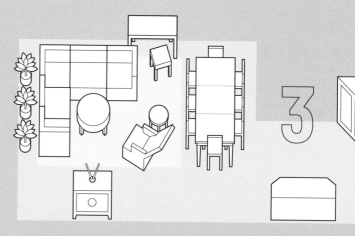

1. To accommodate overnight guests, this room has dual pullout sofas. The ottoman between them works for seating and setting. Two eating areas are also conversation areas. The armoire and desk on the long wall house the elements of a home office.

2. Conversation and TV watching sit at this room's center; a console table hides the back of the TV. A game table makes room for family activities. And the traditional dining room area has a formal, expandable table with plenty of seating.

3. Everything is clustered in the main area of this arrangement. A sectional table and generous harvest table herald this entertaining space and keep the activity centered. The smaller space is devoted to display and storage.

DAYBED

The daybed-turned-guest-bed or trundle bed serves for seating most of the time but opens up to sleep one or two when needed. Look for a style—from humble to sophisticated—that suits your decor and guest-room needs. You'll find pieces like this in many shapes and dressed in a rainbow of upholstery choices.

/ Design Flash /

A plethora of pillows serves as a backrest on this open piece when it sits against a wall. Or put it in the middle of the room to let conversation go both directions.

ARMCHAIR

When it comes to small spaces, the best seats in the house are those that fit—not oversize and hoggish, but still big enough to be comfortable. Choose classic armchairs for a conversation group, but feel free to move one to an office area or, if it's got enough height, to the head of the dining table for extra seating.

/ Design Flash /

The lightweight look comes from the exposed legs. For an even lighter look, choose a chair with open, padded arms.

/THE L-SHAPE ROOM - B Series/

This variation on the L-shape room has two rooms more comparable in size and more separated from each other than the A-series L-shape room. In both configurations, the entrance to the house is at the lower left corner, so a space for coming and going must also be defined; however it shouldn't dominate the area. How separate or how attached you want the spaces to feel can be set by the furniture; just keep a clear path to each space—and to the kitchen and other rooms. A 3-foot-wide path is comfortable for most people to pass through without bumping the furniture.

1. A drop-leaf table easily seats few or many diners but stays out of the way the rest of the time. Two chairs, a sofa, and a love seat offer plenty of seating. The TV can be put in the bunching bookcases, and the chairs moved back for prime-time viewing.

2. Casual, grown-up dining and conversation can take place in either area in this arrangement. The coziest space sits in the area just off the kitchen. The entry is marked by an armoire on the left, a sofa table straight up, and a console table on the right.

3. With angling of the key pieces, the separate areas of the L tend to blend, creating a sense of openness. Tall pieces at the corners anchor the islands of furniture. This arrangement dines six, sleeps two, seats seven, and home-offices one.

ARMOIRE
Be it an entertainment center, a hideaway office, an extra closet, or a family library, the armoire is always a focal point because of its size. Use it to balance a dominant focal point, such as a fireplace. To reduce the visual impact, look for a lower, three-quarter-high version. You'll find choices in new and antique pieces. Size is an issue: Be sure it fits in the door and in the room.

/ Design Flash /
Consider what else this versatile piece can do. Adjustable shelves and dividers allow you to change functions within the box.

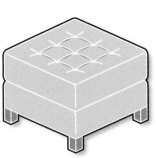

OTTOMAN
The ultimate multi-tasking piece, the ottoman props up feet, serves as a place for setting books and dishes, and provides extra seating. Choose one that pops open for extra storage. Consider weight if you plan to regularly slide it from one place to another.

/MULTIPURPOSE DINING ROOM/

Rare is the small house with enough space for a room solely devoted to dining. Homework, hobbies, and the rest of a home's hubbub often take place in the area designated for dining. Choose and arrange furnishings that allow for several key activities. The result will be a room the family is drawn to every hour of the day. Typically, the dining room is between the kitchen and living room, so keep traffic flow in mind. Think about a table with a tough surface that can handle the range of activities, and choose chairs that do more than sit pretty. In every variation, adequate lighting is important, so add lamps in each work area.

1. The library/dining room has an oval table that floats like an island in the middle of the room. Curved edges create a graceful look that's easy to move around. Bookcases and a breakfront hold precious tomes and china.

2. In the music room/study hall/dining room, the spinet piano finds a home along one wall, and the table tucks into wall-hung shelves. The corner hutch holds books, music, and homework.

3. In the home office/dining room, an extendable table is both work and dining surface. And a bank of bookshelves holds everything. Replace the console table with an armoire if room for a computer is needed.

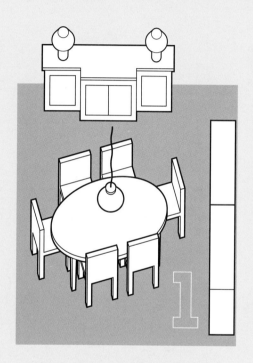
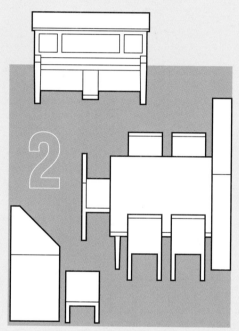
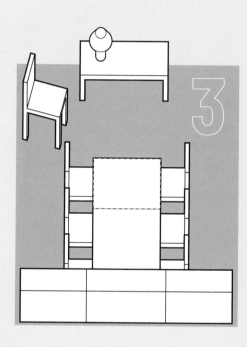

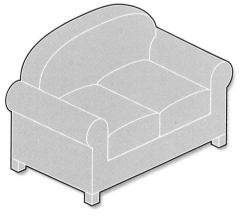

LOVE SEAT
A short, two-seater sofa is more useful and comfortable in a conversation group than the long three-seater sofa. A pair of love seats confirms conversation for four in a small space. Pull up chairs when the conviviality includes a larger group. Pullout models make room for sleepover guests.

/ Design Flash /
Another option is the apartment-sized sofa. Still only seating two, it's a little roomier than a love seat so two new acquaintances aren't forced to be too cozy.

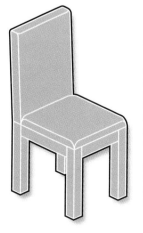

PARSONS CHAIR
This upholstered, armless, slim piece is also called a slipper chair. Flexibility is its main small-house advantage. These chairs move readily from dining room to living room. Simple lines make them adaptable to every decorating style. Choose two to head the dining room table or six to go all round. Or have a couple stationed at the ready in the corners of the room.

/ Design Flash /
For a more formal look, clothe the chair with pleated, to-the-floor slipcovers. Even dressed up, the chairs fit well anywhere.

/DEN-GUEST ROOM/

There's no such thing as a spare bedroom—it's just a space opportunity waiting to be developed. Consider the guest bedroom a chance to create the quiet den, TV room, or home office you've been longing for. The result will be a guest room that makes company feel comfortable and makes you feel good about using the room to its full potential. Don't try to make a small room do too many things. Dual-duty is doable, but the average "spare bedroom" can't accommodate much more activity. The key choice in these variations is mobile occasional tables to make opening up the bed a breeze.

1. A natural accompaniment to all guest rooms is a TV. A pullout sofa allows plenty of room for prime-time stretching out. Tucking a desk in the corner makes a quiet space for writing letters and notes.

2. With an extra chair, the room becomes an additional conversation space. Or turn the chairs for the gang to take in a movie. The ottoman props up feet or holds the popcorn bowl.

3. Wrapping a sectional sofa around one corner maximizes seating and sleeping capacity. Stacking tables spread out to hold drinks and snacks. A good-size TV fits neatly in the entertainment armoire.

ROUND TABLE
Be it dining table, coffee table, side table, or end table, the round shape frees up space and eases the traffic flow through any room. Without sharp corners, there's no fear of painful bumps to passersby. The curves add a lyrical touch, a welcome contrast to the angular edges of most furniture pieces.

/ Design Flash /
When the room is longer than it is wide, consider using an oval or elliptical table. In hallways, try a demilune, or half-round, table to dress up the space.

FLIP-TOP TABLE
When kitchen eating space is limited, a flip-top table can trim down between meals and open out at meal times. No leaves to hide away, no need to pick up the table to move it: Simply flip the top and rotate it into place. This design guarantees that the table will be cleared after every meal.

/MASTER BEDROOM SUITE/

Turning the master bedroom into a suite requires a little ingenious thinking. First, consider how best to free up floor space. Then look for pieces to create a relaxing grouping. Look at chairs and small tables not normally grouped with bedroom sets to expand the spacious feel of the room. For ideas, consider the elements of favorite hotel rooms from vacation trips. The goal is to create a room that has an escape space as well as a sleeping place. Choose bed coverings and window treatments that complement your preferred escape theme.

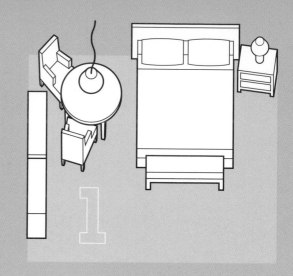

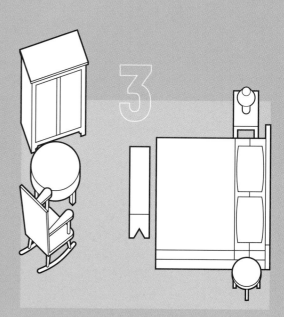

1. Intimate dining or a relaxing cocktail can be enjoyed at the small round table in this suite. Simply tucked in the corner, it doesn't interfere with the room's everyday flow and function.

2. Putting the bed on an angle and using a corner closet significantly change the look of this room. Two chairs group for a quiet tête-à-tête.

3. One end of this bedroom has quite a different feel, with a rocking chair, round table, and angled armoire. This chair is a good choice for relaxed seating.

SOFA TABLE

A console that's slightly lower than the back of a sofa or a pair of chairs can successfully back up a seating group, serve as a room divider, or define the boundaries of a living area. On its own, it works well as a hall piece. to get maximum use from the piece, choose one with plenty of storage below the tabletop. Add a lamp to bring light to the conversation group.

/ Design Flash /
Organize the open space below with three same-size baskets or one large basket. Or use the space to display a pottery collection.

THREE-QUARTER CHEST

To-the-ceiling tall pieces can overwhelm a small room, but waist-high pieces may not provide enough storage. Three-quarter-high pieces offer an extra shelf or drawer of storage space without looming or looking like they'll topple over. Choose pieces with slim lines to keep the visual clutter to a minimum. Pieces that sit up on short legs feel more open too.

/ Design Flash /
Combine chest of drawers and cubed cabinet pieces to create just the right combination of storage.

HINTS & TIPS

/USE YOUR BRAIN; SAVE YOUR BACK/

Moving furniture is labor-intensive, so have a plan before you begin. Not sure how pieces will fit in a room? Use a room-arranging kit with grid paper to do a layout to scale and eliminate guesswork. Or do the same thing in full scale: Cut cardboard templates for each piece of furniture, move the existing furniture out, and move the cutouts around the room until you get a layout that works. At the same time, consider light sources; check to see if there are outlets for lamps where you need them.

/ONE FROM COLUMN A, TWO FROM COLUMN B/

Avoid purchasing whole room sets of furniture. You'll be stuck with their stiff, inflexible arrangements. Acquire furniture one piece at a time, keeping it compatible in style with other furnishings in the house. Then you can move pieces from room to room. Also, before rearranging, take stock of what you have and how you'll be using spaces; then you'll get a better understanding of what you need.

/THE BIG AND SMALL OF IT/

The British have a word for small rooms all decked out in small-scale pieces: twee. And it's not a good thing. Avoid the dollhouse look by choosing one or two significant pieces for each room. These pieces, along with any strong architectural features like a fireplace, help to anchor a small room and give it substance.

/DON'T FORGET THE FOCAL POINT/

The goal of any room arrangement is to create a simple grouping of furniture pieces that work toward the room's purpose—dining, sleeping, working, whatever. Each room should have an architectural feature or dominant piece of furniture that creates the main focus or visual reference point around which all other pieces are oriented.

/DIRECT TRAFFIC/

Pay attention to how people move through the room—and how you want them to move through the room. Eliminate traffic blocknecks by getting rid of extra furniture pieces that stand in the way. Create an easy path through the room without directing it through a conversation group. Allow a path about 3 feet wide where you want traffic to flow.

/ISLANDS OF COMFORT/

Tighten furniture into islands that serve well-defined purposes. Use furniture to define areas within a room. For example, place a console table behind a sofa that sits at a right angle to a doorway. That creates a back "wall" for a conversation group in the living room. An area rug also defines an island of furniture. Or place a seating piece at the foot of the bed to extend the relaxing comfort in your bedroom.

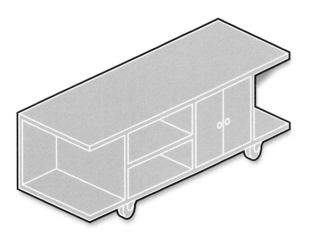

STORAGE ON WHEELS

Roll-around pieces let you put things where you need them when you need them. Wheeled carts, often seen in kitchens, do valet duty in the bathroom or stylishly serve wine in living or dining areas. Coffee tables on wheels can park just about anywhere, and move out of the way for dancing, playing with kids and dogs, or opening the pullout sofa at bedtime.

/ Design Flash /

Wheels that lock hold these mobile pieces in place. Look for mini models that tuck under other pieces to save floor space.

BONUS CHOICES

Murphy Bed

It's gone mod. New models fold into small cabinets or into bookcases. Built-in wall lamps and nightstands make them welcome even in the most stylish homes.

Folding Screen

Divide spaces, display artwork, create a focal point—folding screens are perfect for many decorating options. Look for a model with solid footing to avoid a toppling effect.

Sectional Sofas

Instant conversation grouping. The most versatile styles have individual sections that can function as freestanding chairs.

RESOURCES

BUILDING AND REMODELING

These associations can direct you to professionals who can help you create the perfect small house whether you're building new or updating an existing home.

American Institute of Architects
1735 New York Ave.
Washington, DC 20006
202/626-7300
www.aia.org

National Association of the Remodeling Industry
780 Lee St., Ste. 200
Des Plaines, IL 60016
847/298-9200
www.nari.org

National Association of Home Builders
1201 15th St. NW
Washington, DC 20005
800/368-5242
www.nahb.org

National Kitchen and Bath Association
687 Willow Grove St.
Hackettstown, NY 07840
908/852-0033

Whenever you're hiring someone to work on your home, be sure to get a contract that clearly states both the work to be performed and the fees with a payment schedule. Many firms have standard contracts that they use. Read the contract thoroughly before you sign, and get a copy for your records. All changes should also be in writing and kept with the original contract.

One area of new house design that's of particular interest to people who like small homes is New Urbanism. It's based on the idea of creating neighborhoods, not just blocks of houses. To find out more about this concept, and the new small houses included in these designs, check into the following:

The New Urbanism
by Peter Katz
This book is the cornerstone of the concept.

National Townbuilder's Association
1400 16th Ave. NW Ste. 715
Washington, DC 20036
202/518-6300
www.townbuild.com
Contact this organization to locate existing locations and new locations currently being developed.

DECORATING SERVICES

To find an interior designer in your area, contact:

American Society of Interior Designers
608 Massachusetts Ave., NE
Washington, DC 20002
202/546-3480
www.asid.org

Many stores offer design services along with their products. A firm that offers a full line of furnishings with their design services is:

Decorating Den
19100 Montgomery Village Ave.
Montgomery Village, MD 20886
www.DecoratingDen.com
800/332-3367

FABRICS, WINDOW TREATMENTS, AND WALLCOVERINGS

This list is just a starting point. In addition to these firms, check your local phone book for stores and design professionals that sell these items.

Calico Corners
203 Gale Lane
Kennett Square, PA 19348
800-213-6366
www.calicocorners
This retailer sells fabric, upholstered furniture, window coverings, and bedding. A catalog is also available.

Hunter Douglas
Upper Saddle River, NJ
800/438-4397
www.hunterdouglas.com
A manufacturer of many styles of window coverings.

F. Schumacher
79 Madison Ave.
New York, NY 10016
www.fschumacher.com
Fabrics, wallpaper, carpet, and other home furnishings from this firm are sold under the following well-known brand names:
Schumacher
  800/332-3384

Gramercy
800/332-3384
Waverly
800/423-5881
Village
800/552-9255

Smith and Noble Windoware
1181 California Ave.
Corona, CA 92881
800/248-8888
www.smithandnoble.com
Order custom shades, blinds, and drapes—as well as window treatment accessories (cornices, rods, tiebacks, etc.) from this catalog retailer. Smith and Noble also makes custom rugs. The selection is extensive and the delivery fast.

FURNITURE

You never know where you'll find the right piece—a tasteful end table may be exactly what you wanted for a night stand—so look at everything a manufacturer or retailer has to offer. Also, furniture designed for older children may just be smaller-scale pieces of the same grown-up designs used in master bedroom suites but the youth furniture will be a better fit for small rooms.

Call, write, or e-mail the companies you're interested in to find out how to receive a catalog or locate a retailer in your area.

Ethan Allen
P.O. Box 1966
Danbury, CT 06813-1966
888/324-3571
Fax: 203/743-8298
www.ethanallen.com
A full-line furniture manufacturer with both traditional and contemporary designs.

Ballard Designs
1670 DeFoor Ave. NW
Atlanta GA 30318-7528
1-800-367-2810
www.ballarddesigns.com
This catalog retailer has traditionally styled upholstered and wood pieces.

Bassett Furniture
3525 Fairystone Park Highway
Bassett, VA 24055
276/629-6000
www.bassettfurniture.com
A full-line furniture manufacturer.

Eddie Bauer
P.O. Box 97000
Redmond, WA 98073-9700
800/625-7985
www.eddiebaur.com
Specializes in casual home furniture and textiles.

L.L. Bean
Freeport, ME 04033-0001
800/441-5713
www.llbean.com
This well-known outdoor outfitter now has several lines of casual home furnishings.

Blu Dot
3306 Fifth St. N.E.
Minneapolis, MN 55418
612/782-1844
www.bludot.com
Makes ready-to-assemble, reasonably priced contemporary tables and storage pieces.

Broyhill
Consumer Center
1 Broyhill Park
Lenoir, NC 28633
For a decorating packet call:
800-3BROYHILL (327-6944)
To find a dealer call
877/518-9182
www.broyhillfurn.com
A furniture manufacturer with a full line of traditional and contemporary pieces.

Century Furniture
12th Street Northwest
Hickory, NC 28601
828/326-8201
www.centuryfurniture.com
A full-line of traditionally styled furnishings. Many of the classic wood pieces (dressers, bookcases, and tables) are well-proportioned for use in a small house.

Crate and Barrel
P.O. Box 3210
Naperville, Il 60566-7210
800/996-9960
www.crateandbarrel.com
Originally a home accessories retailer, this firm now also sells a large selection of furniture.

RESOURCES

Design Within Reach
455 Jackson St.
San Francisco, CA 94111
415/837-3940
www.dwr.com
This catalog and online retailer specializes in classic contemporary designs.

Mitchell Gold
135 One Comfortable Place
Taylorsville, NC 28681
800/789-5401
www.mitchellgold.com
A full-line furniture manufacturer. Many upholstered pieces are available with slipcovers for a easy care.

Home Decorators Collection
8920 Pershall Rd.
Hazelwood, MO 63042-2809
800/245-2217
www.homedecorators.com
This catalog retailer offers many specialized pieces of furniture.

IKEA
800/434-IKEA (4532)
www.ikea.com
This Scandanavian furniture manufacturer and retailer has a large selection of modern furniture.

Lane
800/750-LANE (5263)
www.lanefurniture.com
A full-line furniture manufacturer.

La-Z-Boy, Inc.
800/625-3246
www.lazboy.com
Beyond the well-known reclining chair, this company now makes furniture under a dozen company names, including Kindcaid, Pennsylvania House, and Bauhaus USA.

Lexington Furniture
Attn: Consumer Services Dept.
P.O. Box 1008
Lexington NC 27293-1008
800/LEX-INFO (539-4636)
www.lexington.com
A full-line furniture manufacturer. Call or check web site to find a retailer.

Maine Cottage
P.O. Box 935
Yarmouth, ME 04096
207/846-1430
www.mainecottage.com
A manufacturer of brightly painted wood pieces and lively upholstered furniture, as well as wicker furniture.

Norwalk Furniture
100 Furniture Parkway
Norwalk, OH 44857
419/744-3200
www.norwalkmfg.com
A full-line furniture manufacturer. The new Joe Ruggiero Collection is a very adaptable furniture line.

JC Penney
800/322-1189
www.jcpenney.com
The home store has a good selection of furniture, including ready-to-assemble pieces.

Pier One
800/245-4595
www.pierone.com
This home accessories retailer also carriers some small furniture pieces including tables and chairs, as well as accent pieces.

Pottery Barn
800/922-5507
www.potterybarn.com
This catalog and retail firm has wood pieces, side tables, consoles, and arm chairs appropriate for small homes.

Thomasville Furniture
P.O. Box 339
Thomasville, NC 27361-0339
800/927-9202
www.thomasville.com
A full-line furniture manufacturer.

Room and Board
4600 Olson Memorial Highway
Minneapolis, MN 55422
800/486-6554
www.roomandboard.com
This catalog and online retailer carries elegant wood and upholstered home furnishings.

Sauder Woodworking
502 Middle St.
Archbold, OH
419/446-2711
www.sauder.com
Manufacturer of ready-to-assemble wood furniture.

Sears
800/549-4505
www.sears.com
Check the home store for appropriately sized pieces of upholstered and wood furniture.

Target Stores
888/304-4000
www.target.com
This retailer carries chairs, bookcases, tables, and storage pieces sized appropriately for small rooms—as well as accent pieces, such as lamps.

Techline
500 S. Division St.
Waunaukee,WI 53597
800/356-8400
www.techline-furn.com
Sleek, modern storage and office furniture.

Workbench Furniture
800/736-0030
www.workbenchfurniture.com
A retailer with several lines of contemporary furniture.

STORAGE SPECIALISTS

California Closets
1000 Fourth St., Ste. 800
San Rafael, CA 94901
415/256-8500
www.californiaclosets.com
This manufacturer of customized closet organizing systems offers plenty of options for a luxurious and efficient closet.

The Container Store
2000 Valwood Parkway
Dallas, TX 75234
888/266-8246
Retail stores offer hundreds of products for storing just about any item in the home. The web site offers storage solution scenarios for a variety of closets and rooms.

SECONDHAND SPECIALS

Terrific one-of-a-kind buys at bargain prices are just waiting to be found at flea markets, second-hand stores, and garage sales. Check your local phone book to find second-hand and antique stores, and check the newspaper for weekend garage, estate, and tag sales. Also:

The Internet
For a state-by-state listing of flea markets, go to www.FleaMarketGuide.com. The site is geared to flea-market vendors but also has information useful to consumers.

There are plenty of auction and antique sites, including eBay.com, tias.com, and Amazon.com. Since web sites change frequently, you'll find the most current information by using a search engine.

For any internet purchase, as with any store purchase, be sure you understand the terms and conditions of the sale.

INDEX

INDEX